GROW BAG GARDENING

AN ECO-FRIENDLY STEP-BY-STEP GUIDE FOR BEGINNERS

LILY WOODS

CONTENTS

Introduction   vii

1. Welcome to the Wonderful World of   1
   Gardening
2. Getting Started with Grow Bag Gardening   24
3. Maintaining and Nurturing Your Grow Bag   52
   Garden
4. Special Gardening Skills   84
5. Cultivating Root Crops, Vegetables & Fruits in 116
   Grow Bags
6. Cultivating Herbs and Flowers in Grow Bags   140

Glossary   173
Conclusion   183
Resources   185

Your FREE give-away
begins now!

A Special Gift to our Readers

My FREE gift to you is "**How to use readily available Bicarbonate of Soda**" in your garden to get magnificent results. **YES! Your heard right... Bicarbonate of Soda!**

Scan the QR code below to claim your gift!

https://bit.ly/LilyWoodsGardeningSpecialGift

DEDICATION

Special Thanks to my Grandparents and Parents for their giving nature and unconditional love.
Thanks to everyone on my publishing team and illustrator Alessandra Carenzi.

INTRODUCTION

"A garden is a grand teacher. It teaches patience and careful watchfulness; it teaches industry and thrift; above all, it teaches entire trust."

— **GERTRUDE JEKYLL (2011) 'WOOD AND GARDEN: NOTES AND THOUGHTS, PRACTICAL AND CRITICAL, OF A WORKING AMATEUR' CAMBRIDGE UNIVERSITY PRESS**

For me, gardening has indeed been one of my life's greatest teachers. The gardens I had the honour to work on teaching me skills, knowledge, and values I could not have learned anywhere else.

At an early age, I helped my grandparents in their gardens. There was never a day when I didn't stop by to feast my eyes on the brilliant colours of the flowers and fruits that grew abundantly in there. They were simply breath-taking!

Only when I was growing up, I understood why the birds, bees, and other creatures frequented our garden. It became some sort of sanctuary for them, where they can partake of the bounties of nature.

I've carried that love and passion for gardening into my adult life. I have been growing all sorts of plants in my garden, from flowers to fruit-bearing plants, to root crops. I've been teaching and helping others how to start and maintain their gardens for quite some time now.

Yes, you can say that gardening has become my advocacy in life. I want everyone to enjoy the many benefits a garden offers - from having nutritious food right outside their homes, with for picking anytime they want, to have that fresh, sweet fragrance that only a combination of fresh fruits and flowers can provide.

But teaching communities can only get me so far. I want more gardens - all over the world!

That's why I'm writing this book. I want to share my experiences, practical ideas, and research with everyone on white hats to have a garden.

Yes, you read it right - everyone - which includes YOU.

I want you to learn how to produce your food and be self-reliant through simple but proven methods of gardening, without expensive investments in equipment, materials, or even gardening training.

Because gardening is for everyone!

You'll make mistakes, and that's ok. I made lots of mistakes as a new gardener.

- I've tried planting beautiful flowers only to realize that they won't grow in my garden.
- I've over-watered my plants, thinking they need all the water they can get only to see them die in just a few days.
- I thought I won't be able to garden in the city, what with no planting spaces in our apartment
- I didn't know which to plant where, so I ended up planting the wrong plant here and there. The result? Plants that died due to overexposure to sunlight and other elements of nature.

But my grandparents always encouraged me to just push forward. They inspired me to never give up. And I'd like to be that grandparent of sorts to you. I want to be the hand that helps with and inspires you that you can start and grow your garden if you just set your mind to it. I want to be that soft voice that gently nudges you to go on even when you feel like giving up.

Allow me to be your gardening guide and you'll learn:

- Why the lack of space is not an issue if you want to start a garden. There are so many ways to start a garden even if you think you don't have enough space. There are different gardening methods for different garden spaces. I'll be discussing these in Chapter 1. You can also use grow bag gardening which I'll be discussing in detail in Chapter 2.
- The types of plants you can grow. Yes, you can grow any type of plant anywhere, but wouldn't you want to see healthy-looking plants in your garden? And this only happens if you choose the right plants for your area.
- Why the green thumb is just a myth? I've heard this over and over: Gardening just isn't for me. If you want plants to die in 48 hours, tell me to plant. I just can't do it - I don't have a green thumb. Well, I've proven this untrue time and again! You'll learn more about this in Chapter 1.
- Why grow bag gardening is becoming the "in" thing. There are many types of containers for gardening, but grow bags are becoming the most preferred by

more and more people. Why? You'll know in Chapter 2.

- That gardening need not be an expensive hobby. No, you don't need expensive tools or materials for grow bag gardening. Even grow bags are economical! You can create some for your garden.
- And more!

What This Book Is All About

In this book, you'll find a myriad of topics that will help you start and grow your garden!

Here is an outline of each chapter:

In Chapter 1, you'll learn when and where gardening started, the different benefits it offers, along with important information about plants, the myth of the green thumb, and the tools you need to make gardening more effective and enjoyable.

It's all about growing bag gardening in Chapter 2! There, you'll know why growing bags are your best option when it comes to gardening. You'll also learn how to plant in grow bags along with my best practices and common mistakes to avoid.

After reading Chapter 3, you'll be raring to try to grow bag gardening immediately. I suggest you read Chapter 2 first before doing anything, so you'll have an idea as to how to maintain and nurture your garden. Planting is easy - but keeping plants healthy is another story.

And when you've started your grow bag gardening, you'll want to be a better gardener. Of course, you'll need special gardening skills for this purpose. That's what Chapter 4 is all about. You'll learn how to transplant and propagate plants the right way/ I also have tips on how and what to compost - because really, there are some things (regardless if they're organic) that shouldn't be composted.

Which root crops, vegetables, and fruits can you plant in your grow bags? I'll be discussing this in Chapter 5.

Chapter 6 is about cultivating herbs and flowers in grow bags.

You can think of this book as the A to Z Guide you can rely on whenever you need help ASAP. It has everything you need to know about grow bag gardening. Just open the pages and get ready to immerse yourself in my wonderful world of gardening!

WELCOME TO THE WONDERFUL WORLD OF GARDENING

From the earliest of times, our ancestors knew that plants can be a source of food. They gathered nuts and wild berries and dug root crops.

At around 8500 BCE (Before the Common Era), the Neolithic Era, also called the Agricultural Revolution, began. Men started cultivating cereals along with domesticating goats and sheep.

Then, in 8000 BCE, the Neolithic People cultivated different types of crops like wheat, barley, peas, lentils, and beans. This was also the era when the spread of these crops began. There's evidence of their presence in the Danube Basin, the Nile Valley, and so on.

Ever wondered when our favourite corn was first cultivated? It was in 7000 BCE, in Central America. It was also in this era when rice was first cultivated in the Yangtze Valley of China and apples, in Southwestern Asia.

In 6000 BCE, oranges were cultivated in India and the Tigris River Valley.

Through the centuries, gardening became an integral part of men's existence. They relied on it not only for their daily sustenance but also as a source of herbs and spices for their health and wellness.

Gardening became a significant feature in all the great early civilizations, from the Egyptians to the Greeks to the Chinese.

Why Should You Garden?

Let me count the ways. Gardening not only improves our health and well-being; it also provides financial and social benefits. And the best thing? We get to contribute to environmental sustainability in our own, special way.

How does gardening benefit our health?

What's all-in-one stress relieving, memory-enhancing, and mood-uplifting activity we can do daily? Gardening! It has so many other health benefits like:

Guards against Dementia

Researchers at UCLA and the University of Pittsburgh discovered that older adults who engage in physical activities like gardening, swimming, or dancing had 50% fewer chances of getting Alzheimer's.

It's because these exercises increase the volume of some parts of the brain including the hippocampus, which controls memories.

So go ahead, garden dementia away!

Builds Muscular Strength

I'd like to think of gardening as an all-in-one activity that builds my muscles and helps maintain my weight. All that digging, planting seedlings, or watering my plants keep belly fat away, giving me a leaner waistline and well-toned muscles all over!

Boosts Mood and Soothes the Senses

What can be more uplifting than seeing the product of your handiwork? All those green, leafy vegetables, red ripe tomatoes, and peppers, create a picturesque scene that can delight the senses. Add the sweet, tangy, refreshing scents of herbs and spices and you'll have a mood-booster that soothes the senses all day through!

Improves Mental Health

Evidence shows that gardening has a positive effect on our mental health and wellness. Green care, or therapy by exposure to plants and gardening has been found to have beneficial effects on our mood and mental health. Just viewing plants and gardens can reduce stress, fear, anger, and sadness!

Basil

Helps prevent heart disease

Inactivity is one of the causes of heart disease - and gardening can provide you with an avenue to be more active. A study shows that people who do gardening or similar physical exercises have a 30 percent less chance of having a heart attack or stroke.

Eating garden greens also minimizes the risk of heart diseases. The World Health Organization (WHO) mentions that "Current evidence indicates that fruits and vegetables consumed as part of the daily diet can help reduce the risk of coronary heart disease, stroke, and certain types of cancer."

The Financial and Social Benefits of Gardening

Let's say you're a regular basil leaf user. Imagine you have a couple of basil plants that provide you with more than your daily needs. You can dry the leaves and save them for future use or trade them with your friends and neighbours.

And that's for basil leaves alone. What if you have tomatoes, peppers, green leafy vegetables, and other herbs and vegetables that you and your family consume daily? You'll be saving a lot of money!

This doesn't even include the savings you can get from healthcare costs due to all the health and wellness benefits gardening provides.

And that's not all!

Since gardening uplifts, the mood, you'll be spending time on something worthwhile without spending a lot of money as you would when you go shopping or eating out. What a way to lose weight from splurge eating!

And because gardening requires you to bend, lunge, squat, push and pull, you can cancel that gym membership. It's a double-purpose activity amid the sights and scents of fresh herbs and flowers.

Now, if you've enough space in your garden and you maintain its beauty regularly, why not rent it out? You can have it listed on directory sites as a reception venue or a campsite.

Environmental / Ecological Benefits

Helping maintain the natural equilibrium

A beautiful garden does not only attract people. It also serves as an open invitation to birds, bees, butterflies, salamanders, and similar animals. And when your garden has plenty of them, you won't only enjoy the sweet songs of birds or the lovely colours of butterflies - you help balance the earth's natural equilibrium.

Reducing Pollution

Pollution. It's one of the biggest problems our world is facing. People get sick due to the effects of air, noise, and soil pollution. Our health is compromised because of the air we breathe, the food we eat, and the never-ending noise out there.

How does gardening help minimize pollution?

Plants filter the air. Yes, plants can filter the air through photosynthesis. The leaves of plants convert the carbon dioxide that comes from our breath, our vehicles, the appliances we use at home, chimneys, to the oxygen we need to survive. They can also help remove toxic substances from the air we breathe.

Plants are Natural Sound Absorbers

If you're living in a highly populated area, chances are, you are constantly bombarded with noise from all over - vehicles, noisy neighbours and their pets, pedestrians, and occasionally, road excavations.

Help minimize the noises coming from your surroundings by planting hedges and shrubs.

Reducing Carbon Footprint

In everything we do, we release carbon dioxide into the environment. Each time we use our vehicle to buy food, go shopping, or seek entertainment, we increase our carbon footprint.

Imagine adding your carbon footprints to the billions of vehicles that manufacturers use to deliver their products to distributors, then from distributors to groceries and restaurants? Some experts say that the increase in severity of typhoons and floods are the result of global warming and climate change, which are major effects of the increase in carbon footprints.

But did you know that if your garden can replace 20% of the food you buy, you'll be reducing your carbon footprint by approximately 68 pounds a year?

Reasons people don't garden, and the simple solutions

With all the health, social, financial, and ecological benefits of gardening, you might wonder why some people don't do it.

Here are three major reasons why, according to research done by the National Garden Bureau.

Lack of Space

Convenience is probably the best reason why more and more people live in cities. Working people want to be closer to their jobs. Students want to live near their schools. They live in tight spaces with minimal space for gardening. Some residences even have limited access to sunlight and fresh air and no soil to plant on. That's why the people living in these areas choose not to garden.

The solution? Try alternative methods like vertical or container gardening. Vertical gardens save a lot of space because plants grow upward, following a vertical frame.

Now, if you don't have even a small garden plot to plant on, you can try container gardening. This way, you can have plants on your deck or even indoors.

Lack of Time

Some people say they can't do gardening because they don't have enough time to do it. They're so busy raising kids, building careers, and other extracurricular activities.

The solution? Choose indoor plants that don't require much care and attention. Snake plants, spider plants, Chinese Evergreens, and succulents belong to this category. They need minimal water and sunlight. You don't even have to aerate the soil they're planted on often.

Lack of Knowledge or Information

Another factor that discourages people from gardening is the lack of information. They don't have the necessary knowledge on which plants to put together, when to plant, when to water, or put fertilizer, among others.

The solution? Find trustworthy gardening websites. Tree-hugger has a list of websites you can visit if you need information about gardening.

Different Types and Methods of Gardening

When you're exploring gardening for the first time, you might get overwhelmed with all the information out there and the many different options it offers.

I know - been there, done that. Some with great results, others, better to be forgotten because I wasted a lot of time, money, and effort on plants that didn't grow as they should.

Be realistic. Be aware of what you can afford in terms of space, time, and budget.

To help you out, I've listed several types of gardening. It's up to you to determine which is right for you, depending on your available space, the amount of time you have, and the money you can spend on this worthwhile activity.

Traditional In-Ground Gardening

This is one of your best options if you have sufficient space and good soil. It's cost-effective because you won't need pots or other types of containers. You can start one anytime and if you decide to change methods, you can do so without too much hassle.

But beware - because this type of gardening invites a lot of weeds. Unstopped, weeds can threaten or even destroy your plants.

Plus, traditional in-ground gardening needs a lot of water, good soil, and effort on your end. You also need to know how to till the soil in a way that won't hurt your plants and kill friendly worms that keep your soil healthy.

Not to mention that too much exposure to the sun can open your soil to radiation.

If you want to do in-ground gardening, you must first pick a spot in your area, clear the weeds, and treat the soil with the right amount of compost. I'll be discussing composts in a different part of this book.

Container Gardening

What's great about container gardening is that you can start it anytime even if you have limited space. All you need are pots or other types of containers that can hold your plants. And in case you need to change residence, moving them out isn't a problem. You can carry all of them to your next home.

Container gardening looks great wherever - balconies, patios, or even windowsills.

However, you need to have a set schedule for watering your plants as they dry faster. You might also need to change pots when your plants have outgrown their previous containers. Pots can also be another extra custom, especially durable ones.

Spinach, Cucumber and Cherry Tomatoes

Raised Bed Gardening

Raised beds are typically made from bricks, timbers, or wood. You see them in parks, outdoors of malls, airports, and similar areas.

Raised beds may require sufficient space, but they provide better drainage, allowing the soil to dry faster. This is also a good choice for people who suffer from frequent back pain because they don't have to bend low or sit on the ground.

The Downside? Wood and bricks can be a costly expense, so once you set them up, you'll have to think twice about moving them.

Vertical Gardening

If you live in a city where gardening space and fresh food are scarce, why not try vertical gardening? You can set it up on your balcony, patio, or even inside your home.

There are a plethora of vertical gardening setups and containers you can use for this purpose - grow bags and small pots are a couple of options.

However, be aware that not all plants can thrive in this setup. Lettuces and other leafy greens, herbs, and some spices are some of your best options.

Hydroponic Gardening

Is planting on soil, not your thing? Fortunately, there's a way to plant using water and fertilizers without the need for soil, and it's called hydroponics. With this method, you can have a fresh supply of leafy greens and herbs all year round, no matter the weather.

You can have a small or big hydroponic garden anywhere you want.

However, hydroponic gardening doesn't come cheap. It requires a lot of water and fertilizers, the latter being a bit costly.

Aquaponics

Aquaponic gardening is what you'll need if you prefer to have a steady source of fish and greens to eat. You can have some plants floating on top of your aquarium's water (like lilies on a pond). Now, that's what I call double-purpose gardening!

Square Foot gardening

What can you do with a square foot of soil? To a gardener like me, it can be a precious space for growing plants close together sans the frequent weeding. Here are some examples of what you can plant in a square foot, according to North Dakota State University:

- 9 onions, beets, bush beans, bush peas, garlic, or spinach
- 16 carrots or radishes
- 4 lettuce, chard, marigolds, or kohlrabi
- 1 tomato, pepper, eggplant, broccoli, cabbage, or corn
- 1 squash, cucumber, or melon per 2 square feet
- 6 vining plants, such as beans or peas, on trellises

However, square foot gardening requires wooden frames which can be quite expensive as you need to replace them when they start to rot.

Grow Bag Gardening

The heart of this book, grow bag gardening, has been around since the 1970s, but has only recently gained popularity due to its many benefits. Grow bags are flexible and portable, you can carry them anytime, anywhere. But probably its biggest advantage is that it allows air pruning (More on this topic in the succeeding chapters).

Understanding Plants

What plants need to survive and flourish

Like us, plants are living things that need just the right amount of essential care and attention. Their primary needs are:

Water. Some plants need lots of water to thrive, while others can do with a little. Without water, nutrients from the soil cannot pass through the roots. But don't get too zealous about watering your plants as they might die from overwatering. A good rule is to water your plants only when the soil is dry.

Light. Without light, a plant cannot go through the process of photosynthesis. Although the sun is the primary source of light, artificial light can be used as an alternative for certain plants. But like anything else, too much or too little can do more harm than good. Plants exposed to the sun can get sunburned. On the other hand, insufficient sunlight can cause lightening of leaf colour and less dense foliage. Hairy plants will also become hairless due to the lack of sufficient sunlight.

Soil. Think of the soil as a plant's anchor. Sure, some plants can grow without soil, but they will need a frame or similar structure to grow robustly. Plus, the soil is where plants get nutrients from.

Other forms of nourishment. Aside from soil, light, and water, plants also need different kinds of nutrients. They're called macronutrients and micronutrients. Among the macronutrients are:

- Nitrogen
- Potassium
- Phosphorus
- Sulphur
- Calcium
- Magnesium

The micronutrients needed by plants are:

- Copper
- Boron
- Cobalt
- Chloride
- Silicon
- Zinc
- Iron

- Molybdenum
- Manganese

Maintenance and Protection from Destructive Elements

Weeds. Weeds can starve your plants because they compete with them for sunshine, water, and nutrients from the soil. And as you may have noticed, weeds grow and spread abundantly! If you don't stop them, they can damage and eventually kill your plants. So what can you do with them? You can use organic weed solutions like mulching and crowding, remove them by hand once a week, or go the easy way - spray them with weed removers.

Pests. Aphids, gnats, and whiteflies are just three of the insects that can damage your plants. Different pests damage plants differently. Some can cause your plants' leaves to wilt or brown, while others can chew them up, leaving you with ragged-edged leaves. The worst-case scenario is when these pests eat up all your plants' leaves. Without leaves, photosynthesis won't happen. Without photosynthesis, plants will die. How to get rid of them? You can use store-bought or natural pesticides to eliminate them. Another option is to go organic. You can create homemade insecticides using soap and water, or chopped tomato leaves and water, and many more.

Disease. Yes, plants get diseases too. Some of these diseases are:

- Gray Mold
- Powdery Mildew
- Leaf Spots
- Bud Blight
- Early Blight on Tomato
- Blossom End Rot
- Rust
- Snow Mold

All of these diseases can damage your plants. They can also stunt the growth of the fruits of fruit-bearing plants like eggplants and tomatoes.

Adverse Conditions

The Role of Climate

Ever wonder why you can't grow those great-looking tropical plants in your garden? Or you've tried growing it, but it eventually died? Was it your fault?

No, it isn't. It's just that climate plays a huge role in your garden.

This is why you have to know the right plants to grow in your region at the right time of the year. But don't despair - because there are some varieties of plants that can grow in any climate - with some extra TLC. By TLC, I mean taking them indoors during winter so you can prevent them from freezing outdoors.

And here's another thing to consider - due to climate change, a lot of gases are emitted in the air - which warms the planet. The result? Extreme weather changes like intense droughts and flooding.

And with flooding and drought, plants are not the only ones that suffer. The soils erode due to flooding, carrying with it vital nutrients that our plants need.

On the other hand, intense droughts can kill plant life due to the lack of moisture that carries nutrients from the soil to the plants.

Precipitation / Rain

A little rain is good, as it saves you from a day's worth of watering the plants in your garden. And as I've mentioned earlier, water is one of the basic needs of plants. Precipitation can come in the form of rain, freezing rain, ice pellets or sleet, snowfall, or hail.

But what happens to plants when they're exposed to too much water? It can damage plants and compact soil. When this happens, plant roots are smothered and drown.

Too much rain in summer can leach nitrogen out of the soil. And nitrogen is an essential nutrient for photosynthesis.

Too much snow and ice can break twigs and tree branches. The de-icing salts that help prevent ice from forming can also kill plants by burning and dehydration.

Warmth

How much warmth do your plants need? It depends on the recommended exposure to sunlight, moisture drainage, elevation, day and night temperatures, and thermal heat mass.

Different plants react to different levels of warmth. Some thrive on high temperatures, like cacti and similar plants. However, most plants need only about 96 degrees F. (36 C.). A little more warmth can cause their leaves to wilt and brown. Some eventually die.

Read more at Gardening Know How: Does Weather Affect Plant Growth: Effect of Temperature on Plants https://www. gardeningknowhow.com/plant-problems/environmental/ temperature-on-plants.htm

Quality of Soil

The quality of the soil you are planting on also affects plant growth. The question is - what's your purpose for planting? If you intend to plant fruit-bearing plants, then a good mixture of good soil with drainage is your best option. Now, if you want to plant in containers, choose potting soil.

Do you need to have a green thumb to grow a thriving garden?

Ah, the myth of the green thumb! Time and again, you might have heard friends and relatives say that gardening is only for the blessed ones born with green thumbs.

The truth is, gardening does not rely on green thumbs or whatever thumb colour one must-have. There are some steps to follow and concepts to learn, but just about everyone can do it. Everyone can have a "green thumb"!

You just have to have a growth mindset. And to have that, you must be willing to do lots of trial and error. Take notes and learn from your mistakes.

Yes, you might end up killing a plant or two, but that's not the end of the world! Here's what you can do so you make the most out of your trial-and-error gardening:

1. Start a plant journal.
2. Create separate columns for every plant you have.
3. Create schedules for watering, fertilizing, weeding, etc.
4. Write your observations - what are you doing that's working? What's not?
5. Maintain your journal

The Most Important Gardening Tools You'll Need

They say a carpenter is only as good as his tools. Because no matter how good a carpenter is, if you give him an ugly, unworkable piece of wood, he won't be able to create something good.

Similarly, gardening requires you to have a good set of tools. They don't have to be top-of-line tools, though. For me, as long as they can do the job they're supposed to do and are durable enough, then they're good.

So here's my list of tools, in no particular order.

1. **Weeder.** A weeder is a must-have tool for every gardener. Believe me, it can make your life a lot easier. Pulling weeds with your hands isn't a wise thing to do because you might end up with itchy skin. Sometimes, some weeds can even give you minor cuts. I'd advise against weed killers too, especially if you're new at using this. In a small area like a grow bag, weed killers might damage your plants too.

2. **Garden scissors.** Some newbie gardeners think they won't be needing this ubiquitous tool. You'll be needing it for a lot of tasks - opening seed packets, cutting threads, pruning small twigs or flowers - the list can go on. So always have one in your gardening arsenal.

3. **Hand trowel.** This is one grow bag gardening tool that you must have. It's great for digging holes to plant your seeds in, removing weeds, and many more.

4. **Pruning shears.** If you intend to grow fruit-bearing plants in your grow bag garden, then, these shears are something you shouldn't miss. It's because these plants become small trees with hard branches. If you don't have shears, it'll be very difficult for you to cut those branches.

5. **A water hose with a sprinkler or a sprinkling system.** One thing I love about hoses is that you can easily pull them when you need to water plants in hard-to-reach areas. Now, why do I suggest a sprinkling system? What if you'll be out of town for an emergency and no one will be left to water your plants? With a sprinkling system, all you have to do is input your watering schedule, and voila - your plants will be watered without any help from you!

6. **Shovel.** Got some big grow bags? Then a shovel will help you transfer soil from the ground to the bag faster and easier. Just imagine if you'll use a trowel for this purpose - it might take you forever!

7. **Gardening gloves.** If you don't want to end up with bug-bitten, dry and itchy hands, use gardening gloves. They'll protect your hands from pest bites, plant stings, thorns, and thistles.

8. **A small stool.** Save yourself from never-ending

backaches and joint pains by sitting or kneeling on a small garden stool. Just make sure you get one that can support your weight to keep you safe.

Now that you know the basics of gardening, it's time to explore grow bag gardening.

2

GETTING STARTED WITH GROW BAG GARDENING

The What and Why of Grow Bag Gardening

Grow bags enable you to garden without having a garden

No yard space to garden in? Create your garden space! With grow bags, you can garden to your heart's content.

Among the best gardening innovations, grow bags enable urban dwellers and those without or with limited plots to achieve their gardening dreams. Affordable and practical, grow bags are the perfect containers to help create your garden space. Your vegetables and flowers won't know the difference and will reward you just as well.

In no time, the container gardens adorning your patios, balconies, and porches will be a daily source of delight.

Apart from that, the story portion of your yard that was once unsuitable for plants is now bustling with thriving vegetable plants ready for picking.

Why Grow in Grow Bags?

Sturdy and inexpensive

Grow bags are made of porous sturdy fabric. They come in a variety of sizes and shapes. Unlike other plant containers, grow bags are light and some are even equipped with handles.

Grow bags will last anywhere from 1 to 10 years or more. The quality of its make determines its lifespan. It can be reused more often if cleaned well and stored properly.

Space-Saver

Garden containers are space savers. And a grow bag does it better than any other. It can be flattened after washing and stored for the next planting, which can't be done for unused pots, plastic, or wooden containers. Its significant space-saving versatility saves you from the unsightly mess created when plant containers are piled up.

House Plant

Better Aeration and Drainage

With grow bags, plants are happier and healthier.

Why? Because grow bags provide better aeration and drainage. Plants in grow bags do not suffer what their counterparts go through in pot containers. Grow bags are made of breathable materials that provide air supportive of vigorous root growth. The porous nature of grow bags enables natural water drainage and avoids water accumulation that rots roots which is very damaging to a plant.

Prevents Root-Bound Plants

If you observe an unhealthy potted plant even when it is fertilized, it is most likely because nutrients are not absorbed. Roots, as they grow, remain pot bound in potted plants. After reaching the lining of the pot, the roots grow and continue to spiral inside.

Those tangled uproots cause problems with oxygenation and water stagnation when there is inadequate drainage. As a result, the plant is root-bound, which affects its ability to absorb nutrients.

Since grow bags are breathable, the soil by the edges of the bags tends to be dry and exposed to the air. You'd think this is disadvantageous for the plant.

But here then is the awesome part. The roots can detect air and dryness when they reach the side of the grow bag. At this point, the roots realize that this is the end of their growth. This natural occurrence where roots are "burned" off upon exposure to air and dryness is called "air pruning".

Nature wonders that small root tips sprout from roots that were "air pruned". The small -branched- root tips grow and make it easy for the plant to take in water and nutrients. As a result, growth and overall plant health increase. Now, your grow bag contains a vibrant and happy plant.

All the possibilities of gardening without the limitations of traditional in-ground gardening

Gardening is a popular pastime for people who live in homes with spacious yards. They have enviable in-ground gardens that provide a place to grow vegetables and flowers. Traditional in-ground gardening though isn't feasible for apartment dwellers or residents of high-rise buildings or those with no yards.

But what's so wonderful about gardening today is it's no longer limited to methods of traditional in-ground gardening.

Gardening is still possible even for those with no ground space or if you have, it has poor soil quality. These limitations don't matter for those who want to garden.

So take heart, those planning to become gardeners. You can still plant. Using containers. And grow bags are the best choice. You can now enjoy the wonder you've always felt when you saw plants thrive on high-rise buildings, balconies, and even in the nooks inside apartments.

With grow bags, you can place your plants anywhere you like if they receive morning sunlight. You can line them up in any way to create a garden that can highlight a focal point. How about your porch or windowpane adorned with lustily blooming Petti monies? Or your exposed porch trusses providing an anchor for your evergreen drop plants. With grow bag plant containers, you'll be able to express your creativity in a way that will surprise you.

For your poor-soil-quality space that you want to be transformed into an in-ground garden, arrange on it your plants grown in biodegradable grow bags. After harvest, you can dump your grow bag and all that it contains to decompose on the ground space with poor soil quality. Over time, the soil quality will improve. Thus, grow bags are much more preferred - easy to move around, supports aeration and good drainage. They are also reusable and biodegradable containers that are conveniently helpful in the improvement of soil quality.

But a word of caution when moving plants. Move plants where their lighting and temperature needs are met.

Grow bags allow gardening in fresh soil year-round and faster production of crops.

Grow bags with the right soil, proper bag size, correct watering and nourishment allow for faster crop production. The soil that you fill your grow bag with is designed with all the necessary elements to enhance the growth of fruit, vegetables, and flowering plants. And the advantage is that soil from old bags can always be changed with fresh new ones.

Grow bags support a gardening method that optimizes the harvest of fresh produce from a particular area, say in a large grow bag. Interplanting or single planting can work in grow bags with less time and space. You can experiment with planting the same plant at different schedules to assure year-round production of the same crop. Or try planting complementary crops like related salad greens in the same area.

With some experimentation in planting, attention, and proper watering, you will be awed at how well plants grow in these planter alternatives and give you much produce.

Bags enable you to cultivate different crops simultaneously

With your grow bags, you can plant simultaneously. Simultaneous planting involves planting several varieties of either the same or different types of plants with varying maturity dates at once. This means you plant them at the same time the seedlings that have different maturity dates. You either sow the seeds or buy from the nursery. And with the right soil, your container gardening will give you plentiful, variety produce and a great sense of oneness with your plants.

How to choose the right to grow bags for your needs, and where to get them

Now that you've decided to use grow bags for your container garden, here are some considerations to help you select the right bags.

Size

Buying grow bag requires you to consider its size for best plant results. A grow bag's size depends on what you intend to plant. The size of the plant when fully grown, and the root system will help you determine the bag size you should have for planting.

Grow bags range from 1 gallon to over 20 gallons in capacity. It can be more.

If you intend to plant vegetables, make a list of veggies and herbs your family loves to eat. While you may love squash and other trailing plants, they cannot be produced if your container garden is indoor.

For general guidelines about which size of grow bag to choose for common vegetables, fruits, and herbs check this link:

https://growinginthegarden.com/gardening-in-grow-bags-5-tips-for-success/

Material

A grow bag is made of breathable fabric. They can be woven or non-weave. They also come in with added features, such as handles for easy handling and side openings to make transplanting less stressful.

Woven grow bags are made of cloth fabrics called burlap. It is traditionally made from jute, hemp, or flax plants and can have a coarse or fine weave.

Non-weave grow bags are the more popular ones used. They are made from durable polypropylene plastic used in landscaping. Polypropylene is generally considered to be one of the safer plastics and takes 20-30 years to break down compared to 500 years for some other plastics.

Heading over to the nursery, gardening specialty store, supermarket, or looking at online shops for your grow bag? Make sure you have listed what you want to plant, the size of your bags and the fabric material of your grow bag.

But how about creating our own grow bag? After all, gardening is a domain ripe for DIY initiatives.

Creating your own Grow Bags

Making your own grow bags is simple and easy so long as you have a sewing machine. It is economical especially if you need many bags. A medium-sized grow bag when DIYed costs $1.55 in an April 2021 post.

Preparing your own grow bags is no different from the joy of making plant beds or recycling any containers for planting. Sewing grows bags is fun and is no threat to newbies because you are not sewing your party dress.

If you need assistance measuring the fabric you need for bag size, and a sample costing for a grow bag, you can find a helpful guide on this site: http://empressofdirt.net/sew-grow-bags/#sizes.

Here is where you can start after deciding to sew your own grow bags. For your sewing materials you will need the following.

Landscaping Fabric

You can find this in online stores. They are also marketed as weed barrier fabric. For the best price, check your local garden centre or home improvement store. The fabric is made of polypropylene. Look for a double layer with a label that says 2 to 3 oz weight. Any thickness might be hard on your sewing machine.

Thread

There are outdoor threads that are extra strong and made of polyester.

Optional material is 1 webbing for handles. A medium grow bag requires a 1-yard of webbing. You could use your old shoulder bag handles or find some old bags in your nearby thrift shop.

Sewing Steps:

So now you've got your scissors, ruler, and sewing machine, you're all set to go.

Cutting the Fabric

Thankfully the landscape fabric is easy to handle and cutting the fabric is effortless. When it comes to cutting, your size will depend on what you will plant. For example, to make a square foot grow bag cut a length of 4 ft X 1.5 feet width. You are not cutting for a party gown, so for newbies precision in sewing grow bags is not a requirement.

You can make grow bags any size you want, depending on what you will be growing in them. A square foot is a good size. To make a square foot grow bag you will need 4 feet (1.22 m) plus an inch for the seam. For the height, divide the fabric in half. All square ft fabric sewn is a round finished product. It is the length and the diameter that determines the length of the cloth to be sewn.

Sewing the cut fabric

Sewing is very easy. It's all straight stitching to join the edges of your materials. This is true for all sizes.

How to make the bottom of the bag circular, square, or rectangular is the tricky part of the sewing process. You can watch this video for help. https://www.youtube.com/watch?v=oc-2DDbL4kE

What types of plants are ideal for grow bag gardening?

A variety of plants thrive in grow bags. Grow bags however are not suitable for some plants.

Thanks to grow bags you can grow plants you love to have in your vegetable salad, to garnish your dishes and herbs you have with your tea. And they are not limited to veggies, herbs, and fruits. You can plant your favourite blooms too!

So, let's look at what plants thrive well in grow bags.

Plants that have shallow roots and will not grow tall are perfect for grow bags. Shallow roots do not grow as deep as 24 inches (61 centimetres). And the perfect plant height for a grow bag is when they do not reach more than 2 feet above the ground. It's still possible though to grow larger plants in larger grow bags.

These are the most common plants that can thrive well in grow bags. Each category will be discussed in chapter 5 and chapter 6

Vegetables

- Peppers
- Lettuce
- Arugula
- Kale
- Carrots
- Egg Plants
- Herbs
- Spring Onions

For taller vine plans, they can trail down grow bags or grow them upwards with installed plants:

- Tomatoes
- Cucumbers
- Sweet Potato

Onion, Garlic and Ginger

Root vegetables

- Onions
- Potatoes
- Sweet potatoes
- Beetroot
- Radish
- Carrots

Herbs

- Basil
- Sage
- Oregano
- Thyme
- Cilantro
- Parsley
- Dill
- Cilantro
- Garlic
- Ginger

Fruits

- Figs
- Strawberries
- Lemon
- Raspberries
- Melons

Marigold

Flowers

Most flower roots grow to a maximum depth of 18-24 inches. And most can have a height of 8 to 12 inches. They can all grow in grow bags-- daisies, roses, asters, petunias, zinnias, marigolds, and many more gorgeous, colourful flowers. Line them up in your windowsills to give your home a bright atmosphere.

Here's an article for you if you are a beginner on what to try growing first so you can gain experience and confidence in your gardening journey. Note that not all plants can be planted in the same season. It will be helpful to know when to plant what.

Grow Bags Gardening - The Process

What you need

Your planting is about to begin. You already have all that you need - your gardening tools, implements, and your grow bags. We just need to fill in our grow bags with what makes plants grow - soil.

But we cannot just scoop up topsoil from our ground to fill our grow bags. And why not? Or rush to the garden store and grab a potting soil. It is also not smart.

The soil that you will need for your container gardening is light, able to retain moisture and have enough nutrients to keep the plant growing. You can buy this potting soil from a garden centre. You can also mix your soil if you are not sure of what is in the container soil you're buying and avoid chemical fertilizer. For many though, the love of dirtying their hands while creating inexpensive soil is reason more than enough.

Potting Mix, Potting Soil, or Non-Soil Mix

Potting mix, potting soil, and non-soil mix are terms that are loosely and sometimes interchangeably used for the medium in container gardening. It is worth the time to know what the differences are. So let us dive into each.

Potting Soil

Contains ground soil, and compost. It is heavy and may contain minerals and organic matter including other pathogens generally present in the ground soil. It is soil for a ground garden. Ground soil in grow bags is not healthy for plants. It can get compacted, dense, and water-soaked making the growing environment difficult for the roots to grow. There are conditions outside that check some undesirable elements like fungi, in-ground soil. These conditions are not present in growing plants indoors. Also, the microorganisms that aerate ground soil cannot thrive in grow bags.

Non-Soil Mix

Any potting medium with no ground soil. It may not have the three components' plants need to thrive well in a container.

Potting Mix

It is a soilless medium that has all the needed components-fertilizer, moisture retainer, and the light growing medium.

Compared to potting soil, potting mix has a soilless medium and is sterile. It contains organic components like peat moss, sphagnum moss aged bark or coir; and inorganic components like pumice, styrofoam, perlite, and vermiculite. These components are essential to improve the aeration and drainage capacity of the soil.

The potting mix also contains a slow-release starter or continuous fertilizer. It is lightweight and fluffy.

The mixes are typically all-purpose for container gardening. Also, there are potting mixes formulated to meet the requirements of some plants like orchids or succulents to mention two.

When buying potting mix, take time to read the label and find out whether or not it contains these components. Container gardening soil needs to be light, able to retain moisture, and contain enough nutrients to keep the roots healthy and ensure nice vigorous plant growth.

Again, since gardening is an open venue for DIY initiatives, you can make your mix if practicable for you.

What to do - The Steps:

Let us say you are ready and would like to start planting your favourite raw veggie, the lettuce. Our steps to take are the following.

1. Choose the right to grow bag/s for the plant/s.

Lettuce has shallow roots and does not grow tall; it is no more than 12 inches on maturity. Extra small size grows bag will suit lettuce. It holds up to 2 gallons (7.5 litres) of soil. You do not need to make a drain at the bottom of the bag because you chose a fabric to grow the bag that allows natural drainage. This is not true with growing plants made of plastic or any other container.

2. Determine the best position/location where your plants can thrive and set up the grow bags there.

When you consider where to set your grow bag you must also consider the needs of your plant. For instance, while portability is an advantage of using grow bags, plants in nature are usually stationary. Constant moving from one place to another is stressful for any plant. Secondly, the best location to place your grow bag is where your lettuce will receive at least 6-8 hours of sunlight and where it is shaded from the hot afternoon sun. Minimizing growth disruption for your lettuce from the risk of

broken stem or mangled leaves that pets or children can inflict, is one of the factors you should consider when deciding on the location of your plants. And 3rd, consider all the lifting you do, especially for large heavy grow bags.

Plants grow healthily when exposed to sunlight, especially the morning sun. Remember how photosynthesis depends on sunlight? There will be plants that cannot thrive without direct sunlight. Some plants can only thrive in low light conditions. So, before you buy plants, give your area a good look as to sun lighting. Where there is ample sunlight, they most likely will host your grow bag plants.

So, if you want a good supply of lettuce you will have to consider a good location for the lettuce plantation to thrive.

As you do more gardening, you will soon learn that there are full sun vegetables. There will be plants that grow in shade. In our case, the lettuce. It is generally considered to be a full-sun vegetable and will grow more quickly if given as much daylight as possible. It can tolerate partial shade, especially benefiting from it during hot weather.

3. Line the bag with clay pebbles for better drainage.

You might have to add enough chunky perlite or clay pebbles to cover the inner, bottom of the grow bag if you are unsure of your potting mix's drainage ability.

4. Put in the right soil mix/growing medium.

You can now add the mix you either bought or made.

Fill the bag, loosening the medium and shaking the bag to ensure the even spread of the soil and shaping the bag as well. Leave a couple of inches of space from the top.

5. Plant the lettuce seedling.

With help of a trowel, scoop out soil leaving a hole big enough for the entire root of your lettuce seedling. Place your plant in the hole and cover the roots with the soil that was scooped out. The root ball should just be below soil level.

Lettuce

6. Water following recommendations from your plant source then label.

For the growing plants to succeed, you have to check your growing bags daily especially when the weather is humid and hot. Typically, because it is porous grow bags require more watering to keep the medium moist.

Things to keep in Mind:

As with any endeavour, there will be mistakes. Let's look at some common mistakes newbies and even experienced gardeners make when it comes to using grow bags in container gardening. These common mistakes will assist you in overcoming your fears your crops. They will be a tremendous assurance to making the most of your gardening dreams.

A wrong-sized bag was used.

Sometimes, without much thought, we neglect to observe the correct size for plants. Okay, we say we have the potting mix, enough sunlight, and enough moisture. Now the container. Does the size of the container matter?

When planted in a small container, root systems don't have enough room to freely develop thus making growth stunted for a plant that needs a bigger container. When planted in a big container, you have unnecessarily spent much for pot mix and much space roots have no beneficial need for.

A rich resource on appropriate container size interpretations can be found in this link:

https://www.growjourney.com/finally-garden-pot-sizes-decoded/#potsizetable

No or not enough drainage holes.

Plants have three basic elements to thrive well in grow bags; there is aeration in soil, adequate nutrients, and correct drainage. Aeration and adequate drainage are two big advantages of fabric grow bag over any other container. Grow bags do not need to have drainage holes which are usually necessary for non-fabric grow pots. The porosity of the grow bag naturally drains excess water.

Water that stagnates in plant containers due to poor or no drainage rots the roots and eventually kills the whole plant. Disastrous mistake.

Too much filler material.

Some gardeners find that filling a large planter with potting mix is expensive. So, these are what gardeners call filler materials that come in the light like Styrofoam, plant foams, egg trays, or the heavier ones like pebbles, rocks, and packing peanuts. These are filled into the bottom of plant containers taking care that any filler should not be a space for stagnant water, nor hamper water draining out. A felt or landscape fabric is laid over the fillers before the potting mix is poured. Potting mix is separated from filler material this way.

Others view fillers as a drain clog. Water can eventually accumulate at the bottom due to drainage inhibition, which can cause mold and fungi to develop.

The use of filler materials calls for a balancing act; between lessened cost on potting mix against the potential of your plant dying because of possible clogging in the planter drain.

Using garden soil instead of potting soils.

Garden soil is for in-ground gardening and is not for container gardens.

They are dense and compact. With poor aeration and drainage, roots can't be freely developed and could not grow a vibrant plant.

Overwatering

Know your plants. Some like to dry out in between waterings. Others like to be constantly moist.

When a plant is overwatered, the plant is limp, and leaves turn yellow and drop. You may as well replace the drowned plant with a new one. If your plant still looks healthy in its soaked grow bag, move it to a sheltered dry, and breezy spot for the soil to dry out.

Underwatering

Your grow bags have excellent drainage. Be aware that garden mix dries out more quickly than garden soil. Before watering it is best to determine if the soil is dry. You can stick your finger and if your fingertip feels dry, your grow bag plant needs watering. Apply water until you see it draining from the bag or the drainage hole for other containers. Avoid shallow watering. It's more harmful since water can't reach the root systems.

Unlike drowned plants, a limp, pathetic plant that has not been watered might revive after a good watering. Gently poke holes with a stick to allow water to reach plant roots. Then water the grow bag until you see water seep out from the drain.

Here are more watering tips for container plants. And you could also consider a drip system, to manage your watering.

Underfeeding your plant

Sometimes we feel confident that fertilizer in our pot mix will nourish our plants. However, we must remember that roots absorb nutrients quickly. Secondly, nutrient loss occurs with every watering.

Your plants will flourish with supplemental feeding and need fertilizers regularly. Not all plants have the same kind of fertilizer to optimize growth. Some plants need other forms of the formulation. It is best that you also consult the owner of the nursery where you got your plants.

Nature has also meant that plants can feed each other. And gardeners have optimized this by developing what you call companion planting in containers. Plants supplement other nutrient needs of another plant.

Container gardening is one of the best gardening innovations because it makes gardening possible anywhere. It takes time and care, just as ground gardening does. In addition, it is inexpensive. In container gardening, grow bags offer the best solution. But it is not fool proof from the gardening truth that some gardening mistakes take place. But then, "there are no gardening mistakes, only experiments" as you will eventually discover why Janet Kilburn Philips so declares.

Potatoes

Even if we do our best, some plants will flourish, and others will die. It's nature. No matter where you choose to grow your plants, be it in the ground, in grow bags, or any other non-traditional space, growing healthy plants is a rewarding challenge with incredibly satisfying results.

My grow bag gardening best practices

Except for the issue of possible underwatering of plants in grow bags, all the best reasons for using grow bags in container gardening are available for you to succeed as a gardener. Because good aeration helps roots grow healthier, the grow bag is most beneficial for a plant. Grow bags offer the rest of the benefits to the gardener. The bags are affordable and will last more than one planting season. Storage is easy and can be brought out in time for new planting. Depending on your creativity, you can arrange your plants just about anywhere. Since I started using grow bags, I eliminated the need for me to weed the ground where I would normally plant.

5 gal	.66 cf	Single plant
		or a combination of smaller leafy greens.
7 gal	.93 cf	Tomato, peppers, eggplants, woody herbs like rosemary
		A mix of food crops like a cocktail garden (Mint- lemon verbena-rosemary trailing-eucalyptus)
10 gal	1.3 cf	Long season root crops like garlic or onions, carrots, and beets: large herbs or
		small fruit trees, bay tree
100 gal	10.3 cf	Used in place of a raised bed box
		Root crops, large planting of leafy greens and lettuce
200 gal	26 cf.	Used in place of a raised bed box.
		*Same plants as 100gal

I have the immense joy of seeing my plants thrive vigorously in grow bags. My three best practices for rewarding and successful grow bag gardening revolves around the choice of plant and grows bag size, watering and pot mix, and location. They highlight earlier discussions in this chapter.

1. Choose the right size of grow bag for the right plant. First, determine the plant's maturity size. The height of the matured plant will guide you on what size you pick to grow it in. I usually use the large grow bag which can hold up to 10 gallons of pot mix or 38 litres. I make each bag into a themed bag because I can plant different kinds of plants based on the maturity size of each plant. In one bag, I can plant cilantro, onions, ginger, and celery. In another bag, I can grow herbs that can be used for tea or garnish, such as mint, basil, lemongrass, and chamomile, among others. For adequate airflow between plants, be aware of plant spacing. Themed bags are also a great way to package flowers. Trying out different plants brings out your creative side. I plant mint in the edges of my grow bag where my rosal or gardenia thrives, to maximize available space.

2. Since grow bags require daily watering, especially in the summer months, I utilize a grow bag bathtub, which acts as a self-watering reservoir. It's any flat container in which I place the grow bags, and which can hold up to an inch or two of water. It's a simple kind of sub-irrigation. It allows water to find its way up with the nutrients to moisten the roots instead of over-the-top irrigation. This conserves more water and nutrients. It's safer for the leaves and keeps the surroundings dry and clean because there is no runoff. Furthermore, I know my plants will not

suffer from irregular watering when I am out for a few days.

3. The soil mix is never taken from the garden or even topsoil. I purchase my pot mix. Because of the increasing size of my container garden, I am planning to make my compost mix and test out many new mixtures with old pot mixes. Finally, the location of my grow bags is largely dependent on the amount of sunlight, especially morning sunlight. I know which plants do best in full sun and which plants do best only in the morning streak. As I type this, an inner smile appears. They know I know what they love.

Lemongrass

Okay, now you know what grow bag gardening is all about. But how do you maintain it? How can you keep your garden plants beautiful and healthy? Let's go to Chapter 3.

3

MAINTAINING AND NURTURING YOUR GROW BAG GARDEN

Whether you're a beginner or a seasoned gardener, grow bag gardening needs diligence, patience, and zeal in putting to action the best practices to produce optimal results. Plants need care from germinating them until they grow, become lush, and stay healthy.

Giving your grow bag garden utmost care would keep it green and healthy. So, arm yourself with the basics and get rewarded with lush and robust plants that can inspire you.

In this chapter, I'll share with you some essential information on plant classification and proven tips to keep your vegetables, fruits, and even flowers in tip-top shape. I bet that you would agree with me that your grow bag gardening need not be a hit-and-miss endeavor.

Cucumber

Plant Classification: A Quick Guide

The next question, "What grows well in grow bags?" comes to your mind. Choosing the plants for your first grow bag garden is not a random decision.

So, here's a quick guide to help get you started and discover the plants that best suit you.

Plants have distinct life cycles. Some plants go through this sequence of activities in a relatively short time, while others take many months.

Annuals, biennials, and perennials are the three categories in which plants are classified depending on their life cycle.

Annual Plants

Annuals live their entire life cycle in a single growing season.

They germinate, grow, bear fruits or flowers, and drop seeds. Next, stems, flowers, and leaves from the original plant die in a single growing season. Usually, annuals bloom profusely throughout summer until early autumn.

New plants are produced from seeds that germinate in the spring.

Well-known annuals include the following:

Flowers include begonias, cosmos, petunias, zinnias, and purple coneflowers.

Cucumber, squash, parsley, tomato, and zucchini are examples of well-liked veggies.

Types of Annuals

Cool-season or hardy annuals grow best in cool to moderate temperatures in early spring or autumn. They can also get exposed to light frost.

Examples: sweet alyssum, forget-me-not, snapdragon, sweet peas, pansies

Warm-season or tender annuals grow and thrive best in warm weather. It's best to add these plants to your grow bags in late spring, summer, and early fall.

Examples: marigold, petunia, zinnia, coleus, cosmos

Half-hardy annuals are considered the most cold-tolerant.

Since they can tolerate cold weather but not frost, you may plant them in autumn or spring after the last spring frost.

Example: geranium, petunia, baby's breath

Turnip

Reasons for planting annuals

- Annuals come in a profusion of colors and textures, giving you a feast before your eyes.
- In addition to blooming beautifully from the beginning of spring until the first frost in the fall, annuals grow quickly and readily.
- They instantly give you eye-catching garden beds that will drive away your stress.
- In addition to blooming beautifully from the beginning of spring until the first frost in the fall, annuals grow quickly and readily.

- They act as great fillers around a focal plant, emphasize bare shrubs, and brighten up landscaping.
- If you want to have a lot of vegetables and flowers in your garden, annuals are the way to go.
- Spruce up your porches and window boxes with annuals.

Black eyed Susan, Foxglove and Forget me not

Biennials

Biennials complete their life cycle in two growing seasons. They undergo primary growth during the first year - the seeds germinate, and the roots, stems, and leaves develop. In the following year, they yield flowers and bear fruit. However, they do not live long as the perennials. The majority of them perish but some survive to the second season and continue to flower.

Which of the following widely grown biennials would you want to grow?

Vegetables: cabbage, carrots, cauliflower, celery, kale, leek, onion, parsley, turnip

Flowers: Alpine poppy, forget-me-not, black-eyed, foxglove, sweet William

Why plant biennials

- Compared with annuals, biennials have a better tolerance for cold temperature and frost.
- They self-sow easily; you need not reseed every year.
- Since they take more time to sprout and grow, they help improve degraded land, but the wait is worth it.

Perennials

The perennials are known as the backbone of every garden. They complete their life cycle in more than two years. Once they begin to grow, they bear flowers, produce fruits and seeds; and the process continues for three or more years. Together with a few shrubs, trees are all classified into perennials.

Also considered as cold-hardy plants, some perennials bloom only during spring, summer, or autumn. Others rebloom while there are also long-blooming perennials.

Perennial plants require different degrees of upkeep and care. Some may require trimming to preserve their vigor and keep them clean, while others are hardier and require less care.

Here are some well-known perennials:

Vegetables: tomatoes, ginger, asparagus, spinach, horse-radish, garlic

Fruits: peach, lemon, mulberry, grape, strawberry, banana

Flowers: Shasta daisy, hydrangea, goldenrod, daffodil, peony, bleeding heart

Asparagus

Bleeding Hearts and Peony

Why go for perennials

- They are easy to propagate.
- Perennials improve soil condition since their roots help in preserving soil moisture.
- They give your garden design a leafy presence and help to shape it.
- They help ensure that crops are available at different times.

So, think about the plants you'd like to raise. After all, grow bag gardening offers you a fast and straightforward way to have a vibrant and eye-catching landscape.

Choosing the soil

My soil combination consists of 1/3 moss, 1/3 compost mixture, and 1/3 vermiculite to help retain soil moisture.

I take off the wood chips, replace them with new compost with 10-20% organic matter, and properly mix everything.

Prepping up your grow bag

Clay pebbles or chunky perlite should be used to line the bottom of your grow bag. Fill the bottom of the bag with at least 1 inch (2.5 cm) with pebbles or perlite. Doing this helps ensure good water drainage for your plants.

Fill the bag to the brim with soil. By loosening the soil, you can break up any clumps of soil that have formed. At the top of the pack, I leave around 5 cm of space.

Then shake the bag a little to make sure the soil is equally distributed. Pierce drainage holes about half an inch (1.3 cm) apart at the bottom of the bag if it doesn't have any.

Your grow bag is now ready to be planted.

How to water plants in a grow bag

Plants, like humans, require water to survive and flourish. Plants are approximately made up of 80 - 95% water. Without enough moisture, plants would not survive.

Water helps plants in various ways. It helps transport nutrients and organic compounds from the soil and carries them to the stems and leaves. It also aids in the photosynthesis process.

Plants use water to manufacture carbohydrates which they utilize for photosynthesis.

Keep the soil hydrated but not saturated. The plant's roots will not penetrate deep enough into the soil to grow well if the soil is too damp.

I need a moisture meter to measure the moisture level because it's more precise than poking my finger in the soil or feeling around outside the grow bag.

Why is watering plants in grow bags challenging?

Cabbage, Spinach and Cucumber

With inadequate water, plants get dehydrated, wilt, and droop. Meanwhile, too much water can cause their roots to rot. To avoid underwatering or overwatering, you need to know the basics of watering plants in grow bags.

At this point, you may have some queries on watering the plants in your grow bag garden.

Grow bags are porous. What does it imply? First, soil dries out faster in grow bags than in traditional pots. Second, plants in grow bags require more and frequent watering. Third, some grow bags, unlike other types of containers, lack drainage holes.

Remember, you won't either like drowning or under-watering your greens. Thus, you need to find the middle ground so that crops and other plants stay well-hydrated in grow bags. Most plants, however, favor moist but well-drained soil. It means the earth lets water at a moderate rate; there is neither water pooling nor puddling.

Root system. Annuals have shallow root systems. They need frequent watering so they don't dry out. On the other hand, perennials have deeper root systems. It is also worthwhile to know that young plants need more frequent but lighter watering. When their roots grow deeper, the watering interval becomes spread out in larger amounts.

Temperature, humidity, and wind. Plants use more water on hot days. Their water use also increases when the evaporation rate gets higher and humidity decreases.

Stage of growth. Plants use more water as they grow as well as during their flowering, fruiting or heading time.

What plants grow best in self-watering grow bags?

- Spinach
- Cucumber
- Lettuce
- Tomato
- Lemongrass
- Summer Squash

Helpful tips on watering plants in grow bag gardening

- As a rule of thumb, plants in grow bags need more frequent watering since these bags drain fast.
- Water generously but gently.
- Don't overwater or underwater. Too much water causes the plants to get soggy, while too little causes them to become dry.
- To keep the grow bags moist at all times, set up a drip irrigation system.

Drip irrigation uses a slim tube with emitters or drippers that are closely spaced to each other. Similarly, the grow bags are placed close to the plants.

Drip irrigation is simple to install using your current outdoor faucet and some flexible rubber tubing. Each bag has individual emitters that allow you to customize the amount of water given to each plant. Don't forget the timer for no fuss watering.

Using a Self-Watering System

- Start by placing a watering reservoir under the grow bag. Fill it up with water so the plant can wick sit in it up as it needs it. Any container, including a kiddie pool, will suffice. If the container is too deep, however, an overflow will be necessary.
- Using a self-watering tray to give your plants consistent moisture. Each tray can hold a half-gallon of water while the capillary mat provides a steady water supply as they need it. This tray fits one tomato, or one pepper grow bag.
- You may use a grow bag with a watering reservoir or add an olla - a simple, unglazed pot - to the grow bag. An olla filled with water keeps plants alive in a dry climate and during summer.
- Burying the olla keeps the soil around it moist and perfect for plants. It also saves your effort and time since an olla releases water slowly to its roots under the ground.
- You may convert your terracotta pots into simple do-it-yourself olla for your garden. Use an adhesive to seal your pot's drainage hole.
- Alternatively, you might fill the bottom of the pot with roughly an inch of cement. Combine one part

cement, two parts sand, and just enough water to make it moist but not sticky. You'll need around 1/2 cup of cement and 1 cup of sand for a single olla.

- Using a pre-mixed bag is also a convenient alternative.

More tips on maintaining and nurturing grow bag garden

- Choose the right size of grow bag.
- An extra small grow bag holds up to 2 gallons (7.5 liters) of soil. Use this for arugula, basil, calendula, kale, rosemary, sage, and thyme.
- A small grow bag holds up to 3 gallons (11 liters) of soil. Best for beet, carrot, celery, dill, parsley, and strawberry.
- A medium grow bag holds up to 5 gallons (19 liters) of soil. Good choice for beans, broccoli, cucumber, eggplant, ginger, okra, pepper, and turmeric.
- A large grow bag may contain up to 10 gallons of soil (38 liters). Tomatoes and sweet potatoes work well in this.
- Choose plants with "dwarf" varieties or bush types over the vine varieties.
- I recommend planting the following crops: arugula, beet, carrot, cucumber, eggplant, green onion, kale, lettuce, pepper, potato, radish, strawberry.
- On the other hand, plant herbs that also thrive well

in grow bags such as basil, cilantro, dill, ginger, oregano, parsley, rosemary, sage, turmeric.

Carrot

Use the best type of soil, which is a combination of compost, vermiculite, and coconut coir or peat moss. It makes the soil light and airy. Fill your bags with this mix to take advantage of the room inside the grow bag.

- Place your grow bag in the best area according to the amount of sunlight it needs. Most plants require at least 6 to 8 hours of direct sunshine to flourish. Morning sun is preferred, and a little afternoon shade is ideal, especially if you live in a tropical climate.
- Use a high-quality potting medium instead of garden soil. The latter is dense, and it doesn't allow good

water drainage or aeration, resulting in your plants' poor health.

- Select the best location for your grow bag. Use the best type of soil, which is a combination of compost, vermiculite, and coconut coir or peat moss. It makes the soil light and airy. Fill your bags with this mix to take advantage of the room inside the grow bag.

- Place your grow bag in the best area according to the amount of sunlight it needs. Most plants require at least 6 to 8 hours of direct sunshine to flourish. Morning sun is preferred, and a little afternoon shade is ideal, especially if you live in a tropical climate.

- Use a high-quality potting medium instead of garden soil. The latter is dense, and it doesn't allow good water drainage or aeration, resulting in your plants' poor health.

- Select the best location for your grow bag. Most plants thrive in direct sunshine; thus, set your grow bags in an area that receives at least 6-8 hours of direct sunlight daily. The morning sun is best but I recommend to place them where they can get some afternoon shade.

Fertilizing Plants

Fertilizers are considered food for plants. These can be made from natural or synthetic substances containing chemical elements that boost plant growth and soil fertility.

Because most soil lacks vital minerals for best growth, fertilizing your plants is a must. If the soil is not replenished through fertilizers, the yield of flowers, vegetables, and fruits will diminish in time.

Since grow bags require more frequent fertilization, I use half-dose liquid fertilizer every few weeks during the growing season for most crops.

Organic fertilizer

For the most part, organic fertilizer is composed of naturally occurring substances like animal manure and composted organic waste.

They provide garden plants with slow-release, consistent nourishment and make the plants vigorous and self-sustaining.

Since these fertilizers are the products of natural decomposition, they are easy for the plants to digest.

Types of organic fertilizers

Using organic fertilizers has to be managed because they have a burning effect on the plant roots.

Bat Guano

Bat guano is made from the feces of cave-dwelling bats that has collected over time. With its high concentration of phosphorus, nitrogen, and potassium, it makes a good foliar spray.

Bone Meal

Finely ground cow and animal bones from slaughterhouses go into the preparation of this fertilizer. Being rich in nitrogen content, it promotes robust root systems, and it is best used to fertilize bulbs, flowers, and fruit trees.

Fish Emulsion

It is made of decomposed finely powdered fish. Its high calcium and phosphorus content, together with other trace elements, promotes blooming and robust root development.

Manure

Horse, fowl, cow and sheep excrement is used to make manure which is helpful in improving soil quality.

Seabird Guano

Seabird guano comes from the accumulated feces of seabirds. It is rich in nitrogen, phosphorus, potassium, and other trace elements which are beneficial in boosting sturdy roots and in making flowers bloom.

Shellfish Fertilizer

The crushed shells or bones of shellfish and crabs are processed and used to make shellfish fertilizer. It is used to induce flowering as well as to develop the roots of plants.

Inorganic Fertilizers

Inorganic fertilizers, often known as commercial and synthetic fertilizers, are chemically produced from petroleum products or naturally occurring minerals that include nitrogen and other trace elements.

Types of Inorganic Fertilizers

Complete vs. Balanced

A complete fertilizer with the 5-10-5 ratio has 5 percent nitrogen, 10% phosphorus, and 5% potassium whereas balanced fertilizers, such as a 10-10-10 formula, provide equal levels of each nutrient.

The percentages of nitrogen, phosphorous, and potassium on the packages of both types of fertilizers are indicated by the numbers on the packaging. So, the 5-10-5 formula is a complete fertilizer, including 5 percent nitrogen, 10% phosphorus, and 5 percent potassium in it; whereas balanced fertilizers such as the 10-10-10 formula have equal amounts of each component.

Slow-Release and Specially Formulated

For about 50 days or more, slow-release fertilizers slowly release nutrients into the soil. Thus, having fertilizer burn on plants is prevented.

Inorganic fertilizers, on the other hand, are formulated for certain types of plants. They help replenish nutrients in the soil.

Nitrogen Fertilizers

Some examples of nitrogen fertilizers are ammonium nitrate, potassium nitrate, calcium nitrate, and urea, just to name a few of the many available. When applied, these fertilizers have a tendency to elevate the pH level of the soil, making the plant more susceptible to being burned or injured.

Potassium Fertilizers

Inorganic potassium fertilizers, often known as K-fertilizers, are composed of potassium sulfate and potassium nitrate, in addition to muriate of potash, which is also known as potassium chloride.

Use potassium sulfate on plants sensitive to chloride. The non-absorbent potassium nitrate is easy to apply but raises the pH of the soil when applied.

Phosphorus Fertilizers

Use rock phosphate exclusively in acidic soils because the nutrients do not break down in neutral or alkaline soils, making it ineffective for growing plants. Superphosphates have a higher phosphorus concentration than regular phosphates, and they are administered to the roots of plants.

Lastly, ammonium phosphates have high nitrogen and phosphorus content. I apply it when the ground is dry and I always wear a mask and gloves.

All in all, organic fertilizers are environment-friendly, while inorganic fertilizers cause pollution of groundwater, strip the soil of nutrients, and give rise to plant and root burn if not applied correctly.

Inorganic fertilizers deplete soil fertility and reduce soil resistance to pests and diseases when used indefinitely.

Brewing your Fertilizer

With that said, it makes sense that organic fertilizers are the better choice. But before getting them from your garden center, let's discuss why using DIY fertilizers is the best alternative for nurturing your grow bag garden.

You need not buy expensive organic fertilizers. Instead, look around for everyday items in your pantry or backyard, and voila, you are ready to brew your own fertilizer. You not only save money, but you're taking a small step in protecting the environment right in your home.

Now, get ready to "turn your crap into fertilizer, and grow some roses."

Organic Tea Fertilizer

Here are seven ways to prepare organic tea for your plants.

Boiled Vegetable Water Tea

Boil some vegetables in unsalted water. Allow the water to cool. Then pour it on the soil around the plants.

Kitchen Scrap Tea

Use this tea to hydrate your plants. Pour boiling water over plant-based scraps and soak for one to two days in a container.

Yard Refuse Tea

Collect everything from your yard that is pesticide-free - grass clippings, twigs, leaves, and flowers. Store them in a container filled with water for about a week. Then, strain to remove the fragments and fertilize your green buddies.

Compost Tea

Prepare a pail filled with water and add some composted material. Pour water over the compost, cover and wait three to seven days before using it to revitalize your plants.

Manure Tea

Fill a 5-gallon container halfway with well-rotted manure. Add water and leave the mixture overnight. Apply the tea to the soil without letting it get in contact with the plant's leaves or stems.

Boiled Egg Water Tea

Provide calcium to your plants by cooling down the same water you used in boiling eggs.

Seaweed / Kelp Tea

Take some dried cold-water seaweed. Toss it in a container with some water after you've removed the salt from it. Keep it covered with a tight lid. Let the tea steep for at least two months before using it as a fertilizer.

Remember to dilute with water any of the above organic tea fertilizers.

Other Garden Fertilizer Recipes

You can also use any of these easy garden fertilizer recipes to make your veggies, flowers, and fruits healthier.

Liquid Grass Clipping Fertilizer

Fill a bucket with grass clippings about two-thirds of the way. Add enough water and stir the mixture once a day. Set it aside for 3-4 days. Then, press the grass solids through a strainer.
Keep the liquid away from the plant's foliage and apply ½ cup to 1 cup around the roots of each plant.

Molasses

If you're using organic liquid fertilizers, try mixing unsweetened blackstrap molasses along with them.

To 1 gallon (3.5 liters) of fertilizer, add 1 to 3 teaspoons (14-44 ml.) of molasses. Use it as a spray after mixing it with water.

Spraying molasses directly on plant leaves encourages the fast growth of beneficial microorganisms.

Coffee Grounds

To keep your greens healthy, add coffee grinds, add coffee grinds to the base of your plants.

Epsom Salt

For added magnesium and sulfur to your flowers and fruits, mix together a spoonful of salt and a gallon of water and use it to water your plants.

Banana Peel

Looking for potassium-rich liquid fertilizer to spray your plants?

Chop banana peels and mix them into the soil around the base of your plants' roots. Organic material is added to the soil when the peels break down.

Alternatively, soak some banana peels in water for several days to make a spray.

Eggshells

Clean and pulverize used eggshells and add them to the soil. Alternatively, you may prepare a spray by mixing 20 eggshells with a gallon of water. Boil the shells for ten minutes and then leave them overnight. Next, strain the shells and add the water. Spray the solution directly to the soil.

Eggshells contain calcium and potassium that help plants develop roots and increase their tolerance to drought

Vinegar

To ward off ants, weeds, and fungus, pour in a gallon of water and add a spoonful of white vinegar. Water your plants with this solution once every three months.

Pruning plants in a Grow Bag

It is essential to remove particular parts of a plant, such as branches or buds, as well as the roots themselves, in order to encourage plant development. As a result, pruning is an essential gardening skill to possess.

Benefits of Pruning

There are various good reasons for pruning plants in your grow bag garden.

- Sustain or improve plant health
- Reduce or eliminate the pest/disease

- Create a specific shape, height, or width of a plant to enhance aesthetics
- Increase the quantity and/or quality of flowers and fruits produced
- Prepare nursery specimen for transplanting

Basic Pruning Cuts

Listed here are the three most basic pruning cuts you may make. The goal of each cut is to get a distinct result.

Angle the blade at roughly 45 degrees when making cuts that entail going above a growth bud.

Thinning cut

It takes the form of completely removing all of the undesirable branches (to another branch or the trunk).

When it comes to species that bear fruit on short limbs on fully grown branches, this cut is suitable.

It's done to protect a shrub from getting overgrown and out of control by removing branches and allowing air and sunshine into the plant's interior.

This technique discourages suckers and encourages early fruiting by eliminating the entire shoot. Hence, it produces the smallest amount of regrowth possible.

Use it to maintain the natural form of woody plants.

Pinching Cut

Instead of the primary stem, two new stems are created from leaf nodes below a pinch or cut that is made.

Aside from making the plant grow twice as many stems, it also results in a more compact plant.

A soft pinch removes just the uppermost portion (the developing leaves and tip) of the stem, while a hard pinch involves removing a longer part of the stem.

Pinching must be done on more mature plants, woody shrubs, or trees.

Heading Cut

This involves making a cut to a node that hasn't fully grown yet so that it can grow firmly and neatly to replace the lost growth.

A heading cut controls the way the plant grows, preserves the lateral buds, and encourages growth sideways, filling in the plant's interior.

Make heading cuts about one-fourth inch (0.5 cm.) above a bud. When pruning, make sure the bud faces the direction you want new growth to come from. By eliminating the branch's terminal bud, all future growth will come from the bud directly below it.

There will be no further growth on the branch now that the terminal bud has been clipped.

Controlling Pests and Diseases

When you take good care of your plants, you have a high chance of beating pests and diseases that may bring havoc to your garden.

Keep as part of your routine, then, the practice of vigilance. Always closely examine your plants so you could address any problem early on.

Common Garden Pests and Diseases

Learn about the most common garden pests and illnesses, as well as how to combat them.

Aphids

Aphids are soft-bodied insects that drain the nutrient-rich sap from the stems and leaves of various plants, causing them to become distorted as a result of their actions.

Utilizing sprays such as soap-and-water mixtures, neem oil, or essential oils is an effective method of eliminating them.

Mealybugs

White cottony masses on plants, stems, and fruit are common indicators of these soft-bodied wingless insects. Often, they are seen when your plants are over-watered or over-fertilized.

The appearance of these pests may occur if you overwater and overfertilize your plants.

To eradicate this garden pest, make a paste by blending a bulb of garlic, a small onion, and 1 teaspoon of cayenne pepper. Set aside for an hour after combining all of the ingredients in a cup with some water. Dump the solids and add dish soap. Fill a spray bottle halfway with the liquid and use it to spray the plants with it.

Powdery Mildew

Dusty splotches of white or grey powder appear on the leaves and stems of diseased plants and it is difficult to distinguish between them.

Stop powdery mildew on plants with 1 tablespoon baking soda, 1/2 teaspoon liquid non-detergent soap, and 1 gallon water. Fill a sprayer halfway with the mixture and evenly spray all plant surfaces, including the undersides of leaves and stems, with it to get even saturation.

Septoria Leaf Spot

If your tomato plants have been infected with this fungus, you will see little dots on the bottom leaves of the plants as the first sign of infection.

Strawberry

Remove diseased leaves by burning or destroying them. Mulch around the base of the plant. Water the plants into their roots early in the morning. Using a soaker hose lets them absorb water slowly.

To prevent the infection from spreading, you may use a fungicide if your plant is severely afflicted.

Slugs & Snails

Mollusks, such as slugs and snails, have a soft exterior and a hard shell. Snails have a protective hard shell, which is their only distinguishing feature from the other mollusks.

They like to eat young, tender plants like basil, lettuce, strawberries, and tomatoes.

Make a beer trap. Slugs will be attracted by the beer's aroma and will fall into the hole, where they will become trapped. Bury half a container near vulnerable plants and half fill it with beer.

Prevent ground beetles from devouring your slugs by keeping the edge of the container 2-3cm above the surface of the ground.

Other than that, I build barriers with things like broken eggshells, pine needles, and prickly cuttings, then recycle the leaves.

Drip irrigation helps keep pests away by reducing humidity and wetness. It also reduces slug infestation while conserving water in your grow bag curtain.

Whiteflies

Like aphids and mealybugs, whiteflies are insects with a soft body and winged wings. They feed most on the undersides of leaves especially during periods of prolonged warm weather.

For whitefly eggs and nymphs, spray 1 oz/gallon Neem oil with 1 oz/gallon water on all leaf surfaces (including undersides). You can also use insecticidal soap, which is made by mixing 1 tablespoon of Castile soap with 1 quart of water.

Remember, plants that are well-cared for not only thrive; they flourish.

4

SPECIAL GARDENING SKILLS

As your garden grows, you'll have more seedlings than you can handle. So, you'll have to know how to transplant and propagate your plants. If you don't, your garden will be so crowded and messy. This can greatly affect the growth and propagation of your plants.

Transplanting

Transplanting is very vital to your plants. There are many signs you can check if your seedlings are ready to be transferred or to be transplanted.

Transplanting is when you move seedlings or small plants from their nursery pot into the garden soil or container like a grow bag. Before you do that, you have to consider the type of soil you need to use for your plants. Also, don't worry if you have a small space, that's okay, but of course it is better to have a larger space to grow more plants in the area.

Before you're ready to transfer your plants outside, you must follow these basic tips and do it correctly.

Prepare your Gardening Tools

Having the right tools especially if you're a new gardener will make a difference in maintaining a beautiful garden.

Scissors

If you're transferring a small plant to its new home from a small bag or plastic seedling trays, you need scissors to carefully cut the bottom portion of the bag or the side of the plastic tray. Make sure that you don't cut the roots of your plant.

Shovel

Its small, rounded edge and body will allow you to move your plant from one place to another. You can use this also for digging the soil, pushing it down onto its back edge.

Spade

Spades are different from shovels. These are big tools for bigger plants. The square edge allows you to till the soil as deep as you need.

Garden Trowels

These are handheld shovels of different sizes. It can also have flat, curved, or scoop-shaped blades.

Your tools are now ready, you can now transplant your plants to their new home.

How to Transplant Your Plants?

1. Prepare the container where you're going to transfer your plant. Knowing the right size of container for your plants is necessary to grow your plant healthy.
2. Put some soil on the container, at least half of it. Another way is to fill your container with enough soil. In the middle, dig a hole enough space to put your plant.
3. Remove your plant from its pot.
4. Inspect the roots. Loosen the soil a little bit.
5. Place the plant in the container and add more soil to cover the roots.
6. Water the plant.

4 Reasons Why Your Seedlings Died

If you are producing your food, it is better to start from seeds.

1. There is no fertilizer

If you're first sprouting your seeds, you need fertilizer to give them enough nutrients to be healthy and grow their leaves.

2. Waiting for the plant to grow big before transplanting it.

You need to transplant your little seedlings into a larger pot after it grows 2 to 3 true leaves. Don't wait until your plant grows big.

3. Failure to harden your plant

If you did not properly harden your plant by taking them outside for enough sun, shade, winds, and outside temperature, your plant won't be strong enough to grow.

4. Too Excited to plant or Transplant

When is the best time to transplant?

Transplanting depends on the plant itself. If you start your plant from seed, it is best to keep track of your plant when it starts to grow its true leaves. Don't rush your plants. There are plants like tomatoes and peppers that are very susceptible to cold temperatures. It is safe to keep them indoors and keep an eye on your local weather forecasts before transplanting them.

Other plants like spinach, radishes, lettuce, onions, and cabbages are cool-season vegetables that are best planted before the temperature gets too warm.

Here are some vegetables and the best time to plant them:

Cool-Season Crops

Cauliflower

The indoor growing time before transplanting: 5 to 6 weeks
Germination time: 10-21 days
Temperature range for best germination: 70-80 degrees Fahrenheit
Best Growing Temperature: 60-70 degrees Fahrenheit during the day and 55-60 degrees Fahrenheit at night
Seed planting depth: ¼ to ½ inch
Outdoor planting space: 18 inches
Days to mature: 50 to 72 days

Onion

The indoor growing time before transplanting: 9 to 11 weeks
Germination time: 10-15 days
Temperature range for best germination: 65-80 degrees Fahrenheit
Best Growing Temperature: 60-70 degrees Fahrenheit during the day and 45-55 degrees Fahrenheit at night
Seed planting depth: ⅜ inch

Outdoor planting space: 12 inches

Days to mature: 60 to 115 days

Celery

The indoor growing time before transplanting: 10 to 12 weeks

Germination time: 21 days

Temperature range for best germination: 60-70 degrees Fahrenheit

Best Growing Temperature: 65-75 degrees Fahrenheit during the day and 55-65 F at night

Seed planting depth: ⅛ inch

Outdoor planting space: 9 to 12 inches

Days to mature: 120 days

Cabbage

The indoor growing time before transplanting: 5 to 6 weeks

Germination time: 10-12 days

Temperature range for best germination: 70-80 degrees Fahrenheit

Best Growing Temperature: 60-70 degrees Fahrenheit during the day and 50-60 degrees Fahrenheit at night

Seed planting depth: ½ inch

Outdoor planting space: 18 inches

Days to mature: 60 to 110 days

Broccoli

The indoor growing time before transplanting: 5 to 6 weeks
Germination time: 10-14 days
Temperature range for best germination: 70-80 degrees
Fahrenheit
Best Growing Temperature: 60-70 degrees Fahrenheit
during the day and 50-60 degrees Fahrenheit at night
Seed planting depth: ¼ to ½ inch
Outdoor planting space: 18 to 24 inches
Days to mature: 50 to 72 days

Warm-Season Crops

Tomatoes

Tomatoes

The indoor growing time before transplanting: 5 to 7 weeks

Germination time: 7 to 10 days

Temperature range for best germination: 70-80 degrees Fahrenheit

Best Growing Temperature: 70-80 degrees Fahrenheit during the day and 60-65 degrees Fahrenheit at night

Seed planting depth: ¼ to ½ inch

Outdoor planting space: 18 to 24 inches

Days to mature: 50 to 90 days

Aubergine / Eggplant

The indoor growing time prior to transplanting: 7 to 9 weeks

Germination time: 10 to 12 days

Temperature range for best germination: 75 to 90 degrees Fahrenheit

Best Growing Temperature: 70-80 degrees Fahrenheit during the day and 65-70 degrees Fahrenheit at night

Seed planting depth: ¼ to ½ inch

Outdoor planting space: 24 inches

Days to mature: 50 to 75 days

* * *

Eggplant, Leek and Round Peppers

Peppers

The indoor growing time prior to transplanting: 6 to 8 weeks

Germination time: 10 to 12 days

Temperature range for best germination: 75 to 85 degrees Fahrenheit

Best Growing Temperature: 70-80 degrees Fahrenheit during the day and 60-70 degrees Fahrenheit at night

Seed planting depth: ¼ to ½ inch

Outdoor planting space: 18 to 24 inches

Days to mature: 55 to 80 days

Watermelon

The indoor growing time prior to transplanting: 3 to 4 weeks

Germination time: 6 to 8 days

Temperature range for best germination: 75-95 degrees Fahrenheit

Best Growing Temperature: 70-90 degrees Fahrenheit during the day and 60-70 degrees Fahrenheit at night

Seed planting depth: ¾ to 1 inch

Outdoor planting space: 18 inches

Days to mature: 65 to 95 days

Squash

The indoor growing time prior to transplanting: 3 to 4 weeks

Germination time: 7 to 10 days

Temperature range for best germination: 75-95 degrees Fahrenheit

Best Growing Temperature: 70-90 degrees Fahrenheit during the day and 60-70 degrees Fahrenheit at night

Seed planting depth: ¾ to 1 inch

Outdoor planting space: 18 inches

Days to mature: 42 to 65 days

Knowing the Tools, You Need in Gardening

Before you're ready to transfer your plants outside, it is important to know these basic tools that you need to help you in preparing your plants.

Prepare your gardening tools.

Having the right tools especially if you're a new gardener will make a difference in maintaining a beautiful garden.

Scissors

If you're transferring a small plant to its new home from a small bag or plastic seedling trays, you need scissors to carefully cut the bottom portion of the bag or the side of the plastic tray. Bear in mind that you make sure to carefully cut the bag and keep the roots of the plant intact.

Propagation

Do you want to multiply your plants for free? Why not try plant propagation?

Many types of plants can be multiplied using inexpensive, simple procedures, and techniques depending on the type of plant.

Plant propagation is the process of multiplying your plants. You can create new plants from existing ones using different techniques. It also refers to the biological reproduction of plants.

Types of Plant Propagation

1. Sexual plant propagation - produces a new generation of plants like planting seeds from the original or parent crop. Use grow bags and the right mixture of soil when multiplying plants through propagation.

2. Asexual propagation is used in the reproduction of plant life like cuttings and grafting. Some plants can be multiplied and propagated in water. The most common plants that can be reproduced are the Aroid and Araceae plants. The best examples are ZZ plants, pothos, philodendrons, and monsteras.

Materials needed to prepare:

- The plant to propagate
- Scissors/pruners
- Glass vessel filled with water
- Garden gloves

Follow these simple steps:

- Step 1: Look for a mature vine with a tiny brown root node below the leaf or stem. You need to cut with a few inches allowance. You will notice after how many days that there will be new roots growing on it.
- Step 2: Remove any leaves near the node that might submerge in water
- Step 3: Put the plant cuttings in your glass vessel and make sure it receives enough sunlight
- Step 4: Check root growth every week and replace water when needed. The water should be clean for healthy root growth.

After 4-6 weeks, and once the roots are 1 inch long, you can transfer them to the grow bags, with enough water and indirect light.

Here are the basic factors to consider in propagating your plants.

1. Check for healthy plants.
2. Consider the most appropriate method, timing, and growth stage of the plant.
3. Protect plants from direct sunlight and heat to prevent them from dying
4. Extra attention and care are required during this phase.

Benefits of Plant Propagation:

1. Create new plants for your garden
2. Save money - it helps increase your savings instead of buying again
3. A great giveaway to family and friends during special occasions
4. Satisfaction and pride once you successfully multiplied and created a new plant
5. Some varieties are limited, and you can do this on your own

Techniques:

The key techniques for propagation are:

Leaf cuttings - you can produce new plants by cutting the mature leaf of a plant. Most of the plants that grow roots from cutting the leaves will have fleshy, thick leaves that mostly grow in clusters. Examples of these plants are African Violet, peperomia, gloxinia and begonia.

Procedure:

1. Stem cuttings - often used for ornamental and fruit-bearing trees
2. Simple layering
3. Air layering

Simple Layering - stems attached to the plants are capable of forming roots. A layering technique develops propagation by bending a branch of the plant to the ground, adding some soil in the middle portion, and then anchoring it in place.

Procedure:

1. **Make a Cut**: From the tip, about 3-5 inches, make a 1/2 to 3/4 inch cut through the stem.
2. **Dig a Shallow Hole**: Slightly bend the branch of the plant. Make sure that the cut portion is directly bent into the soil.
3. **Cover the Stem:** With enough soil, cover the

portion of the stem and make sure to leave at least 6 inches to 12 inches above the soil.

4. **Bend**: In a vertical position, bend the tip of the branch. With the use of a brick or a landscaping pin, keep the branch in position.

5. **Support the Cut**: You have to keep the cut of the stem open by inserting a small stone or pebble. You can also use a match stick or a toothpick.

You will notice that roots will be coming out of the bent stem. Keeping the moisture in the area where the bent is, will eventually develop the roots. Remember to always monitor your plant. In a few days, you will see well-developed roots and this will be an indication that you can already cut the branch away from its parent plant. Now, you can transfer it to a different location or into a different pot.

Air Layering - Thick-stemmed plants or houseplants are ideal plants where we can use this method of propagation. Eucalyptus, lemon trees and other citrus trees are best for this method of air-layering. This process of propagating is creating new trees or shrubs from the stems of the parent trees or shrubs.

You will need the following to perform air-layering:

1. Knife or a sharp hand saw
2. Thread made of cotton, should be thick
3. Polyethene paper or plastic sheet

Procedure:

1. Identify the Branch: The branch should be suitable, healthy, and free from any pest attacks. You will know the best time to do this method of air-layering when you see that there are new leaves growing 0n the plant.

2. Choose the best branch. It should never be too young or too old.

3. Choose the best spot on the branch. There should not be old or mature leaves on the branch where you're going to do the layering.

4. Be sure to cut the branch deeply. Cut the branch using a sharp knife or a hand saw. Make two cuts with one inch to one and a half inch apart from each other.

5. Peel off the Bark: remove the peel ring of bark circularly and expose the inner part of the branch.

6. Cover the part of the bark that has been peeled off with soil. Make about a handful of mixed soil. Form it like a ball. Support the soil with your hands to keep it in place. You can use a mix of wood ash, tree moss and soil for better results.

7. Wrap: Wrap the soil with a polyethylene paper or plastic of your choice and tie it on either side by a cotton thread. Keep it dry. Make sure that there won't be air or water that can enter it.

Lemon Tree

You'll notice that it may take up from one to two months before the roots will appear. Once the root system forms on the stem, you can now do the cutting of the stem right below the bottom of the branch where we wrap with soil. Now, you can pot the layer. Transfer the plant or the layered branch into the ground soil, pot, or grow bag. This new plant will need special care. Take care of it until you see the well-developed root system.

Composting

Learning how to compost is the best way for your organic discards to go on waste. You can produce valuable soil that is rich in nutrients. It is a process of recycling waste materials such as leaves, woods, and food scraps that we generate at home to form a fertilizer that enriches the soil and plants. If it is done correctly, it is very simple and easy to do. You'll notice that there will be no smelly odour in the process.

What are the Benefits of Composting?

1. Composting provides environmental benefits. Your organic wastes in the kitchen won't add up to the pile of wastes in the dumping site. There will be a lot less garbage if you compost.
2. Compost materials condition the soil, add nutrients, and maintain the moisture of the soil which is beneficial to the plants. It gives your garden good organic nutrients.
3. It allows us to turn our waste into something practical for our yards. Recycling food and organic waste materials into compost helps in conserving water since composts have water-retaining capacities.
4. It has a connection with our health. If we do compost, we give back to the soil the benefits we got from it. Thus, the more we compost, the healthier the harvest of fruits and vegetables.

5. Finished compost which the gardeners called black gold can be mixed into the soil and be used as fertilizers.

There are three key ingredients in composting: greens, browns, and water. Make alternate layers of green material and brown materials then add water to it to make compost.

What can you compost in your backyard?

- Coffee grounds and filters
- Eggshells
- Fruit and vegetable peels
- Leaves / dry leaves
- Teabags
- Saw dust
- Nutshells
- Houseplants
- Paper
- Grass clippings
- Old potting soil

What not to compost and why?

- Coal, charcoal - There are substances on these materials that can be harmful to plants
- Meat bones, Fishbones, and Scraps - these create odour problems and will attract pests like flies and rodents.

- Pet wastes - these might contain parasites, bacteria, or viruses that can be harmful to both your plants and to humans
- Dairy products - these also create odour and attract pests like flies and rodents.

What are the methods of home composting?

You can compost both indoors and outdoors. If you have a bigger space in your backyard, composting is the best way to keep your food scraps, falling dry leaves, and other yard debris not go into waste.

Here are the two main types of backyard composting:

1. passive or cold composting
2. active or hot composting

Cold Composting

Cold composting takes longer before you can use the compost. This process is considered "cold" because there are no heat reactions as the organic wastes decompose. If you have a small space, mostly those that are living in condominiums, it is best to do cold composting. It also has minimal intervention by just letting nature do its job in decomposing the organic waste materials. It will take about twelve up to twenty-four months before you can get the usable compost, depending on your method. You can do a cold pile and wait, or you can add-as-you-have-waste materials pile. Do not put diseased plants on your pile because without high temperature to kill the pathogens; fruit flies, maggots, and fungus gnats will come your way.

How to do cold composting?

Pick a Location

Set your compost bin in an area where there is no direct sunlight or in a warm corner of your garden, but make sure it is not too hot. This will be more protected from the elements that will dry your compost out. It is a good idea if you place your compost bin not too far from your house.

Build or Buy Your Bin

Using a compost bin is the simplest and cheapest way to compost if you have a small space at home. You can buy bins at the cheapest price, or you can build your bin. You most probably have these materials at your house that can be converted into a DIY bin. You may have to drill holes along the sides of the bin to allow the air to flow. Ensure that the openings and holes are small enough to prevent the entry of other animals like rodents and snails.

Ideal materials that you might already have at home that you can use as compost bins can be these items:

- Garbage cans
- Wood pallets
- Wire mesh

- Old drawers
- Plastic storage bins
- Wine crates
- Pail
- Add Your Layers

Start your pile with the browns like dried leaves, eggshells, papers, and then layer it with your greens. It would be best to have a pile of leaves on your top layer to keep the pests out of the pile. Make sure to break the larger items into finer pieces for faster decomposition. You can keep on adding green and brown layers in your bin at least once or twice a week until it is full.

Add Water

Check your pile for moisture. You need to add enough water to keep the level of moisture in your compost. Enough moisture and warmth may help speed up the composting.

Collect Your Compost

Compost should look like a dark brown material that smells good and moist before you can remove your pile and collect it to add to your soil. How long depends on the air temperature in your area. You can check after 4 to 6 months or as long as one to two years.

Use Your Compost

You can add your compost and mix about 50% of it and 50% of soil for best results. It is best to add it to the soil when planting ornamental plants, vegetables, shrubs or trees.

Hot Composting

Hot compost is the best and easiest way for backyard composting. This compost pile can break down quickly into black gold for your garden. If you have room for a compost file, choose an area in your yard that has some shade, so it doesn't dry out. You can build your hot compost pile and create a DIY compost bin using a wire mesh.

How to build an inexpensive hot compost bin?

You will need the following:

- Roll of wire mesh ½ inch, 3 ft. tall
- 4 pcs. 4 ft. T-posts
- Roll of Bail wire
- Tape measure
- Small clips
- Hammer
- Cutter

The ideal size of a hot compost pile is 3 ft. x 3 ft. x 3 ft. In this size, it will generate enough heat and will break down a lot quicker.

Here's the Procedure:

1. Prepare your tools and materials.
2. Start with the T-posts. Drive the T-post in one corner, make sure it is sturdy.
3. Measure 3 ft. from the T-post. Do the same procedure on the next corner.
4. Now you'll have 4 corners with the use of T-posts.
5. Wrap around the wire mesh on the T-posts.
6. Take the end of the wire mesh and make sure to wrap it around on one end of the T-post.
7. Cut a piece of the bail wire and secure the end by putting it around one end of the T-post and twist it. Do the same in the middle of the T-post and another one on the bottom part.
8. Cut the ends of the bail wire and ensure to bend the ends.
9. On the other end of the wire mesh, make sure it extends enough to cover and serve as the door of your compost bin.
10. Tie the other corner using the bail wire on the other T-post and the wire mesh. Tie using a bail wire on the bottom, middle and on the top of the T-post.
11. For the door of your bin, bend a small part of the other end of the wire mesh to make sure that there are no sharp ends on it.
12. To close the door, you can cut at least 3 to 5 inches of

your bail wire to tie one end of the wire mesh door to the other side.

How to make hot compost at home?

Like in the cold composting process, you also have the key ingredients for your hot compost: greens, browns, and water.

1. Build your compost pile, making the layers of "browns" and "greens". The first layer should be your browns. Prepare your dry leaves and dry branches at the bottom. This will keep the compost with enough air and moisture.
2. Water the bottom layer.
3. Add your food scraps, coffee grounds, and tea bags.
4. Add a layer of eggshells
5. Water it down again.
6. Do another layer following steps 1 to 5. Make sure the top layer is your brown, dried leaves.
7. Cover the compost bin with a tarp or any plastic cover to keep your compost free from unwanted pests.
8. Turn your compost weekly.
9. Check the temperature of the pile. The best temperature for hot compost is within 135 to 160 degrees Fahrenheit.
10. Check if there are insects or unwanted pests that go around your compost.

11. Check the smell of the pile. You will know that you have done it right if you will get a good earthy smell once you turn and smell it.

No matter how big or little space you have for your garden, you can still have that precious black gold that will help your garden to be very productive and grace you with plants full of organic nutrients.

Composting Toilet

What is a composting Toilet?

It is a device that turns solid waste into compost. This is not the usual type of toilet. You can find it in boat houses, RVs, cabins, or tiny homes. It is similar to a regular toilet but with a different structure for composting human wastes, sometimes called "humanure" in the context of gardening. It does not require connections into septic tanks or sewer systems. There is no flush, the composting chamber is just right below the toilet seat. Operators of these composting toilets add absorbent carbon material such as coconut fibre, untreated sawdust, and peat moss. These additives serve as a microbial starter to ensure that the composting bacteria are in process and include odour prevention.

Potting Mix

This mixture is a soilless blend of ingredients ideal for plants that you can grow in containers or grow bags. It looks like soil, but it doesn't contain real soil. These mixes are more lightweight than the garden soil, have better draining, and are easy to handle and consistent as always.

Preparing your soil is vital to growing a productive garden. The best of it all is that you can make your inexpensive potting mix. You can make your garden soil and prepare your hands to get dirty!

How to make your Potting Mix?

Using good potting soil is an essential ingredient for growing your plants. Using a potting mix develops better results which have plenty of nutrients and good drainage.

Ingredients:

1. Peat Moss

This is mostly composed of moss. It doesn't contain harmful microorganisms that you may find on processed compost. It has a measured acid pH that's great for ornamentals, camellias, and blueberries. You can add lime to balance the pH: ¼ tablespoon lime per gallon mix.

Alternatives

Coco Peat

It is made from the husks of coconuts. It is a better alternative, unlike acidic peat moss. It has macro-nutrients, is more resistant to diseases, and has superior water-retaining capacity.

Leaf Molds

Leaf Molds are very high in carbon but low in nitrogen. If we will give enough time and moisture, decomposed leaves are the best materials that can be added to the soil.

Cat Litter

It is an alternative for plants that don't need as many nutrients as other plants. This is best for cactus, succulents, and bonsai plants.

Wood Fibre

Composted wood fibres can be used as a replacement for peat moss or can serve as an extender for peat moss. It increases the wettability of the mixture. Make sure you do not use treated wood materials.

2. Perlite or Vermiculite

Perlite is a lightweight granular material that gives multipurpose additives to your plant. It is white and like small bits of polystyrene that are made of volcanic glass. It is useful in plant propagation, encourages water to drain through, and is a good hydroponic medium.

Vermiculites are spongy, light, and can improve drainage of the soil. It is made from flattened dry flakes of silicate material which is spongy, light, and it improves drainage. Its colour varies from a golden brown to a dark brown material which is sometimes hard to tell if you are mixing it into your soil. This helps retain some water in your plants.

3. Compost

This is the product of decomposed organic materials. It is created by the natural decomposition and chemical processes which are good for soil amendments.

4. Manure from Livestock

This contains faeces, urine, bedding, and spilled feeds from livestock. This must be processed to remove impurities so you can use it safely. You need to mix animal beddings to this compost. It can be done by doing the process of composting.

How can you create your potting mix?

You will need the following:

- Peat moss or coconut peat
- Compost or well-rotted manure
- Perlite or Vermiculite
- Epsom salt (2-4 tablespoons for a 5-gallon bucket mixture)
- Large container to mix the ingredients

You can start with a 5-gallon bucket mixture for each ingredient and use salt for 2-4 tablespoons. You don't need to worry if there are not enough materials or ingredients, you can just divide the mixture into half or less.

Trellis

These are the frameworks on which crawling plants and some trees are trained. Creating trellis will train the plants especially for crawling plants to crawl it vertically. If you worry that your plants will fall over, these trellis will help to give support and strength to your plants. Trellis is available in the market; however, it is not practical enough to buy because they are expensive.

Why buy pre-formed trellis while you can make your own?

To build your trellis, envision the perfect structure and design for your plants. You can make it more personal, fully functional, and elegant. You can make inexpensive trellis using some fencing and stakes that you probably have a lot of in your yard.

Here are some ideas for your DIY trellis:

1. Wire Wall Trellis - you can use stainless steel tension cables, eye hooks, and anchors to support your self-climbing plants. You are free to create the design of your trellis.
2. Bamboo Trellis - this is best for a vegetable garden. You can form three bamboo sticks like a tepee and tie them with tie twine.
3. Coat Rack for a Garden Trellis - you need an old

coat hanger, either craft it on your grow bags, pots, or attach it to your wall.

4. Garden Tools Trellis - if you have old broken tools like rakes, hoes, shovels, or spades, sharpen the ends and tip them over. You can arrange them directly to the soil, tie them together or use salvaged woods to design and connect them.

5. Attach Trellis to Your Fence - Jazz up your backyard fence with clematis trellis that will support your climbing flowering vines.

6. Pergola - You can make your pergola in your patio or deck as trellises for your crawling vines.

7. Honeycomb Trellis - You can use a mitre saw to make a hexagonal cut and create this lovely, shaped trellis that can be screwed on your wooden fence or walls.

8. Wire Mesh Trellis - Choose the 2-inch classic hexagon chicken wire and form a trellis vertically, attached to a stick or a small aluminium pole.

9. DIY Cage Using wood, steel, or aluminium poles - all you need are four poles and aluminium wire. You can put the poles in four corners of your plant container and use an aluminium wire to tie them together to make a cage.

10. Cattle Panel - you can cut a cattle panel to maximize your garden space and just put it behind your plants.

Be creative, you can decorate your garden using materials already available in your backyard. You can see how amazingly beautiful your decors can make your garden unique.

Gardening skills require patience, passion, and knowledge to make your garden and plants thrive using grow bags. You can plant anything in grow bags, like vegetables and different plants, you just need to be sure what kind of process you will do when transplanting and propagating them. You can produce and do your mix to make sure your plants have the proper nutrients using organic materials which help the environment and saves money. You're sure it is free from any pesticide that might affect your health while having fun and fulfilment in producing your plants and vegetables for your consumption or your business.

5

CULTIVATING ROOT CROPS, VEGETABLES & FRUITS IN GROW BAGS

Benefits of vegetable home gardening

I've always enjoyed keeping a garden in my home, it brings me a different kind of peace and joy. I find that there is a certain pride in growing my food, knowing exactly how my food is grown and what goes into it. I love sharing the joy of gardening with everyone so I thought I would share a couple of benefits that may give you that extra nudge to get you working on cultivating a beautiful and sustainable garden that's sure to be a healthy and fun experience:

Better nutrition

Freshly harvested produce in your garden when you need it means that your vegetables won't lose that many nutrients. The thing about grocery store produce is that it has been picked and transported from different countries or states, these fruits and vegetables have lost a lot of nutrients along the way before getting to your nearest supermarket.

Control over your Crops

Genetically Modified Organisms or Non-Genetically Modified Organisms? Chemical pesticides or homemade pesticides? These are things you usually look into when purchasing your products in the market to ensure that you're getting great quality products and to know what exactly is going into your body. The best part about growing your food is having control over what you grow and what you put in.

I feel much better growing my produce and knowing that my family is eating crops that are up to my standards.

Saving Money

Fresh fruits and vegetables can be quite pricey in the market, especially when they're non-GMO and organic. Having your produce will also save you money by having you skip out on certain areas in the produce section of the supermarket.

You may spend some money purchasing your brand-new grow bags, seeds, soil, and fertilizer but you'll save a lot more money and a healthier lifestyle in the long run if you keep at it. Now that's what I call a worthy investment!

Physical Exercise

Having to pull weeds, bend up and down to expect my produce, and dig in the dirt with my trowel has kept me moving and toned my muscles more than my morning walks. I've also read that the University of Arkansas has published that digging in the dirt can help improve your bone density, now that's a bonus!

Just make sure to watch your form when performing all these exercises to avoid injury! For example, make sure to squat down when you're lifting something heavy to avoid back injury.

Grape

Vitamin D Bonus

Vitamin D is also known as the "sunshine vitamin." By staying outdoors in the sun to tend to my plants, I get a great mood boost by getting more vitamin D. Did I also mention that this vitamin is also an essential vitamin for your bones, teeth, and muscles? Talk about a bang for your buck and this is all from just standing in the sun!

Better Sleep

Because gardening takes so much physical effort and uses up all the muscles in my body, I've had my fair share of falling into such a restful sleep as early as 9 pm only to wake up feeling sore the next day from all the exertion!

The best part? Burning all those calories doesn't even feel like a chore because I'm doing something I love.

Emotionally and psychologically rewarding

I've found that caring for the plants in my garden has given me an extra sense of purpose. According to research, gardening has been proven to help people reduce more stress than reading a book for 30 minutes! Not only do you move your body and take care of your physical health, but you also take care of your mental health. Talk about multi-tasking!

Protect your Memory

It's comforting to know that there is recently published evidence-based research that shows that gardening can help your cognitive functions. So now whether I'm digging, planting, or watering my garden, I feel at ease knowing that my brain is receiving benefits that can help keep dementia away. Now I can garden my worries away while also ensuring that my memory stays in tip-top shape.

Becoming a part of a new community

I've met some of my closest friends through gardening and even learned my best tips from my neighbours. The gardening community is filled with people from different cultures, different generations, and from all walks of life. Learning how to garden and grow your food is a great way to start a conversation with someone new! Who knows you may just be exchanging tips, recipes, and even produce by the end of the conversation?

What I love about the gardening community is everyone's willingness to help. A community that grows together, stays together.

Self-Care

I've learned how to take care of myself better when I started gardening. I've learned to take a lot of breaks when the sun is extra hot, I've learned to listen to my body whenever it tells me I was working too hard, and to applaud myself whenever I accomplish a task. Having all that quiet time to myself while tending to my plants has also given me time to check in with myself and sometimes, I even use my gardening time to meditate.

Gardening has taught me how to have a better relationship with myself and for that, I will always be grateful to gardening for teaching me that lesson.

A Learning Experience

I find a lot of lessons while tending to my garden. Every season yields a different set of crops, and a new set of crops comes with a new set of guidelines for your plant's growth.

Gardening is a constant learning experience for me, and I do believe for everyone as well. I was once a beginner just like you, but with time and patience, I was able to learn something new on how to keep my plants happy and healthy while also improving my inner and outer self.

I find that new seasons and new years bring about brand-new lessons that I can grow from, and I would love for you to find the same joy in gardening as I have.

Why use Grow Bags for your Produce?

Aside from all the advantages of grow bags discussed throughout this book, certain fruits and vegetables do well when cultivated in grow bags and there are specific reasons for this:

- Grow bags promote a healthy root system which is a great advantage for root crops.
- Some grow bags give you the option to access your

produce without removing the entire product from the bag. This feature can save you a lot of time and effort to ensure that your product is ready for harvest, this is especially helpful for products that can no longer be replanted once brought out of the soil.

- Grow bags encourage air pruning which means that roots stop growing once exposed to air. This means that the roots of your plant will be forced to create new healthy roots, giving your plant a healthier root structure. I swear that the crops that I grow in my bags have turned out much healthier than those that I planted in my plastic pots.

- Some vegetables are fast-growing. Combined with the convenience of growing bags, it could mean continual fresh harvest in an easily maintained space.

- Certain fruits and vegetables have small root systems which means they only need small spaces to grow. Grow bags have a variety of sizes that can best suit this need.

- Certain vegetables like cauliflower and cabbage can tolerate crowding, which means that it's possible to have more than one crop in a single large grow bag.

- Some root vegetables rely on depth, not the width of space, making a fabric garden the ideal garden.

- With grow bags, vegetables and fruits are readily available for harvesting and you can place it wherever you find is the most convenient for you!

You can place it near the kitchen or on the patio or the balcony.

- Grow bags release up to 30 degrees more heat than your regular plastic bags, this will keep the good microorganisms in your soil alive inside and give you better produce!
- Grow bags can help prevent overwatering because the fabric can absorb the excess moisture.
- Grow bags are usually made of fabrics that are breathable and allow air to circulate much better. Better air circulation means the roots can absorb water and nutrients much better.
- I find that I'm able to create pockets of ecosystems in every grow bag by planting different crops in the same grow bag. I try to ensure that the crops I plant will not steal each other's nutrients and instead help each other grow.
- If you're renting out an apartment and have no garden space or if the area where you live has bad soil, you can still grow delicious and healthy produce through grow bags.

Crops to plant in grow bags

There is a wide variety of plants that thrive in grow bags. I've listed a few down that's easy to propagate to help you narrow down your choices:

Potatoes

The ever-versatile potatoes, you can mash them or turn them into fries or even bake them as is, they're also easy to cultivate in grow bags.

This versatile tuber will thrive in deep grow bags because they need a lot of depth to flourish. They enjoy cool temperatures, a regular watering schedule, and at least 6 hours of sunshine daily.

I highly recommend not overcrowding these tubers together when planting and keeping the stems constantly covered in soil to ensure its healthy growth.

Radish

Radishes are an absolute gem to have in the garden. This low-calorie root vegetable that's vitamin c packed is very easy to plant, and they are sure to add a pop of colour to any garden they grace.

Radishes are quick to harvest and don't need much space to grow, so I tend to grow them in a shallow grow bag. I keep the grow bag's soil moist and give these vegetables at least 6 hours in the sun.

Whenever I have an excess of radishes, I pickle them and leave them in the fridge ready for whenever I need that palate cleanser in between meals.

Carrots

This superfood comes in a variety of colours ranging from orange to purple, black, and sometimes even white! I love snacking on this vegetable as is but sometimes I shake things up by eating them with a bowl of hummus. Carrots are jam-packed with fibre, potassium, and vitamin a. These deliciously sweet root vegetables rank low on the glycaemic index and are sure to be beneficial for those with Diabetes.

I find that carrots are one of the best crops to cultivate in grow bags because they thrive when planted in them. These crops benefit greatly from grow bags because they need to be planted quite deep into the soil to be able to accommodate its roots. Carrots also enjoy plenty of sunlight, about 8 hours minimum, and can grow from as early as summer up until fall. I recommend growing carrots with beans and squash.

Onions

I tend to use onions for most of my dishes so I tend to go through them very quickly, which can get quite costly when I purchase them from the supermarket. Therefore, it's an absolute must for me to have these bulbs growing in my garden at all times to save on my grocery bill.

I find that the best onions to plant in grow bags are green onions and smaller variety ones. This kitchen staple relies on depth to grow beautifully, and they will thrive in your bag if they have at least 6 hours of sunlight daily. Onions grow best in cool weather, and they can tolerate a bit of crowding, so keep that in mind when you're getting ready to plant them.

I recommend growing onions with tomatoes.

Lettuce

I've found that I'm able to grow an entire salad garden in one large grow bag. This trick saves me space and keeps everything I need for a healthy appetizer for dinner in one space. This leafy green is packed with calcium, potassium, and magnesium and is over 95% water, which means that it's a great source of hydration for your body.

Growing lettuce in your grow bag is very easy and they grow well with other vegetables due to their short roots. This vegetable grows extremely well during the cool weather, coupled with a lot of water, these leafy greens will thrive. To keep your lettuce productive after it matures only picks out the outer leaves so that they can regrow.

I recommend planting your lettuce with carrots to maximize the space in your grow bag or you can plant it with some herbs to keep pests away.

Cabbage

Cabbage

This leafy green that is the main star of any coleslaw can come in a variety of colours ranging from green, red, and white. Cabbage is a nutrient-packed vegetable that's a low-maintenance plant, they will flourish in grow bags.

Plant your cabbages in a shallow bag to help them grow nicely because of their short roots, while also keeping in mind that they only thrive when the weather is cool. These greens love the sun but will also grow just fine with partial sunlight.

Tomatoes

These berries are a staple in any restaurant you'll find, from tomato sauce in pasta and pizzas down to ketchup, tomatoes can be found everywhere. I usually just chop up a tomato and add it to my salad, however, I've recently found out that cooking tomatoes increase the number of key nutrients you can get from them.

I find that tomatoes when cultivated in grow bags need to be planted a little deeper into the soil to grow strong roots. This fruit grows well with at least 6 hours of sunlight a regular watering schedule.

I highly suggest that you try adding a tray beneath your growth bag to promote self-watering, tomatoes are the type of crop that is sure to benefit from this practice. I also suggest that you have a tomato cage set up and ready to go for this plant when it starts to thrive.

I recommend planting your tomatoes with onions.

Cauliflowers

Whenever I need an extra boost of nutrients, cauliflower is my go-to vegetable because of its high number of vitamins. Research also shows that it's low in calories and is high in fibre. I love that this vegetable is a bit sweet, and I think it makes a great side dish. I usually turn my cauliflower into rice.

This vegetable may grow wide, but they do have shallow roots making it easy to plant with other crops in grow bags. Cauliflowers need about 6 hours of sunshine daily and will only need you to water them whenever their soil feels dry.

Chili Peppers

Chilies

I love having these berry fruits on hand so that I can add an extra kick to any dish I'm making whenever I need it. This fruit is a great source of antioxidants and may even help you burn fat. My favourite part about chilis is that they're easy to grow!

Chilies will only thrive in warm temperatures and while they only need a small container to flourish, they do require a lot of sunlight, at least 7 hours. Once you have your chilies set up, make sure to water them just enough to keep their soil moist.

Beetroots

These beautifully coloured stem tubers have quite several remarkable health benefits ranging from them being a great source of nutrients like fiber and vitamin c to having a very low-calorie count.

I find that beetroots are also one of the best crops to cultivate in grow bags because they need the depth to grow a robust network of roots. These taproots will grow beautifully in cool temperatures coupled with at least 6 hours of sunshine daily.

Bell Peppers

These beautiful fruits are composed mostly of water, come in a variety of colours, and are loaded with nutrients and antioxidants, especially carotenoids.

This crop loves the warm weather and is a great addition to any garden. They grow just like chilies with their love for warm temperatures and moist soil. However, unlike chilies, bell peppers love space and can grow very tall, which means having a stake on hand would really help with its structure.

Bell peppers come in different varieties and if you don't feel comfortable growing a tall one, you can opt to look for a type that won't grow as high.

Egg Plants

These big and plump fruits are known for being versatile. There are different varieties of eggplants that are available in the market, I find that the learner eggplants are perfect for cultivation in grow bags. This crop enjoys the warm weather and will most likely need that extra support from a stake to help it grow beautifully.

Eggplants grow well with beans.

Arugula

These delicious greens are one of my favourite products snacks for my salad. These fast-growing greens have a knack for the cold weather, are easy to grow, and taste amazing in salads with their smoky and complex flavour. Arugula or rocket thrive when they get at least 6 hours of sun and have moist soil. I harvest them when they're at least 3-4 inches long. You can choose to either pull out the whole plant or just clip the outer leaves and keep the crown intact so that it can grow again.

Kale

I have been making my kale chips for some time now and I find that my homegrown kale chips taste much better than the store-bought ones! I also enjoy making new flavours for my chips now and then.

Kale is an easy crop to grow and what I love about it is that I can have a steady supply of them throughout the year because they thrive in cool weather, so the only time I may be lacking in Kale is when it's midsummer. These versatile green plants love having at least 8 hours of light and likes its fertilizer, and its water.

Summer Squash, Cauliflower and Parsley

Squash

This is one of my favourite vegetables, they're sweet, nutritious, and a versatile crop in the kitchen. Believe it or not, squashes can be grown out of a grow bag. When I plant squash, I like to have a trellis ready to support the weight of this crop so that it grows happy and healthy. Aside from that, I ensure not to overcrowd them when planting, to give them at least seven hours of sun daily, and to grow them during the warm weather.

Zucchini

One of my favourite courgettes, zucchini is a vegetable loaded with vitamin A, antioxidants, and may even help reduce your blood sugar levels! It's delicious, extremely easy to incorporate into different meals in your kitchen and grows extremely well in grow bags.

I like to ensure that my zucchinis grow in a container that's at least 12 inches deep with a drainage hole. This crop loves the warm weather and the sun, they would grow amazingly well if exposed to at least eight to ten hours of it.

I would recommend reading a stake or a tomato cage because this crop will have long vines and would appreciate the support.

Broccoli

Steamed broccoli is one of my favourite side dishes for any meal, it's a great source of fibre and protein. Broccoli tends to have a widespread, so I like to make sure that I only plant 1 in a 5-gallon container. This crop likes growing in partial shade and cool weather.

Okra

Lady's finger, another name for okra, is well-known for reducing the risk of diabetes, heart disease, stroke, and cancer with its rich resources of vitamin a, c, and antioxidants. When I plant okra, I make sure that the bag I will be using is at least 3 gallons. Okra loves the sun, so I make sure that these have at least 7 hours of sunlight and lots of water. I grow them when the weather is warm, and I find it best to pick them when they're at about 4 inches in length.

Sweet Corn

I have a guilty pleasure of slathering butter all over my sweet corn and eating it straight out of the cob, but now that I have it right in my garden, I won't have to wait until fall to have this treat. Sweet Corns when fully grown can reach up to 12 inches wide and over 12 inches deep, this crop loves its space. I like to choose a variety that doesn't grow beyond 4 feet to keep my garden compact. This crop tends to cross-pollinate quite easily so I grow them around other corn plants. I plant this crop during warmer days and give them about 7 hours of sun daily along with lots of water to keep their soil moist.

Beans

I love having beans around the house because they're a great quick addition to my stir fry whenever I need an extra crunchy texture to it. When I plant beans, I plant them during warmer seasons, when they grow quickly, and I make sure to have a trellis ready to support them as they grow as well. This crop needs about 6-8 hours of sun, and they love water. I harvest these when I see that they're about 8 inches long.

Beans grow great with sweet peas.

Beans

Peas

This crop may be small, but it packs a lot of nutrients, this humble little seedpod is known for being a great source of vitamin e, c, antioxidants for your immunity, and zinc. Although some they may find that growing this crop can be quite troublesome, it's safe to assume that it's worth the trouble.

Peas need a lot of space to grow, their roots go fairly deep into a grow bag, so I usually plant mine in a large grow bag with canes or sticks ready to help the vines grow nicely. This crop thrives in warm temperatures, full sunlight, and a lot of watering

Spinach

I find spinach to be an extremely versatile vegetable because I can use it for a variety of dishes in the kitchen, and it also grows fast so you can have a steady stock of spinach before you know it. This crop grows great in cool weather, full sunlight, and moist soil.

Cut the spinach leaving the stem so that it can regrow once again.

Swiss Chard

Swiss chards are beautiful greens that have violet stems and will add that pop of colour to any garden, but the great part about it is that it's loaded with nutrients and is easy to cultivate in your grow bag.

Swiss chard's root system is quite shallow and will thrive in cool temperatures. This plant prefers to grow in the shade and can tolerate some crowding. It's a very low-maintenance crop.

Cucumbers

I love having cucumbers in my garden because I can use them in my kitchen for salads and smoothies or I can also cut up a few pieces to help moisturize my eyes.

Cucumbers need a big grow bag to have a wide root system. I always have a trellis ready for this crop because it grows vertically. I also try to have it set up in a self-watering planter because this plant loves water. Cucumbers thrive in hot weather and with at least 7 hours of sunshine daily.

Strawberries

Strawberries are one of my favourite fruits, they're rich in vitamin c, fibre, and they taste delicious. I like to turn my luscious strawberries into jams, eat them with whipped cream, or add them to my smoothies. Thankfully, this juicy fruit is easy to cultivate in grow bags, it is a low-maintenance fruit. It just needs rich soil, a lot of suns, and cool weather to grow.

Raspberries

I love raspberries, these nutritious pick-me-ups are easy to grow as well. Raspberries enjoy the full sun and cool environments. I like to make sure that a trellis is on hand when cultivating this crop and that I water it to keep it moist.

I find that raspberries grow great in grow bags because they're quite invasive and this way, I can control their growth and keep them from spreading to other plants.

Blueberries

Blueberries

This delicious superfood is one of my favourite snacks. They're beautiful throughout the seasons and are much easier to handle when in grow bags. One key factor in propagating them nicely is that you keep the pH level of the soil acidic. This crop loves humidity and cool weather.

Blueberries grow great with herbs like basil and thyme.

Cherries

Ground cherries are delicious golden sweet-tart fruits that aren't that well-known. This crop enjoys warm temperatures and at least a full 6 hours of sun! These golden cherries are only ready to eat once they've fallen off onto the floor. These fruits don't do well in cold temperatures.

Warning: The fruits of ground cherries are edible however, the stems, leaves, roots, flowers, and fruit husks are toxic to people and animals. Please make sure to keep these out of reach from your furry friends and family.

Things to keep in mind to make the most of vegetable gardening using grow bags

- Terracotta pots are quite troublesome to move because they're so heavy, this is why I prefer my grow bags. Grow bags are so easy to move and they don't weigh as much as your pots.
- One thing I like about growing my produce in grow

bags is that I can reposition my plants frequently to give them the optimum amount of sunlight and air. I end up getting much better produce and yields because of this advantage.

- Throughout my experience with grow bags, I've found that they absorb more heat than other kinds of plant containers or bags, which means that I have to water my crops more often.

- Grow bags last about 3-5 years and so I consider them to be investments and so, before I purchase grow bags, I make sure that I've already planned for it by figuring out what I will plant in them.

- I find that some vegetables need plenty of fertilizer to grow beautifully, a good example of these would be tomatoes and cabbages. I recommend creating your vegetable feed, as you've learned in the previous chapter, to save more money in the long run.

- Some fruits and vegetables, like tomatoes and eggplants, need support structures to help them grow vertically. I find that it's best to plan my garden layout ahead of time to be able to save space, especially when it comes to crops like that.

CULTIVATING HERBS AND FLOWERS IN GROW BAGS

There are many plants you can grow in grow bags, but for beginners, I recommend those that are easy to grow, and of course, those that are beneficial. Herbs and flowers are two which fall in those categories.

Herbs in Grow Bags

Herbs in grow bags epitomize the concept of portable gardening as you can move them around depending on the season. Transfer the bags under the shade when it is too hot, bring them indoors when the weather is not favourable, and put them out under the sun where most of them thrive.

Terragon

Herbs do not require that much space. Most of them are non-woody plants with small and shallow roots. They grow to up to 9 to 24 inches – higher for some when not trimmed – and with leaves spread diameter of 12 - 24 inches.

They grow well in any type of container, but the most ideal is the breathable grow bag for better control of moisture in the soil. You can have the bags on your balcony, porch, just outside your kitchen, or anywhere around your backyard where you can enjoy them.

You can even plant two or more herbs together in a bag to maximize the space, but you have to make sure they share the same growing requirements.

In this chapter, you're going to learn about some of the best herb options and why they are ideal for grow-bag gardening, as well as processes for getting the best results or output.

Benefits of Growing Your Herbs

Not only are herbs easy to grow; cultivating your own provides numerous benefits:

Healthy and Tasty Addition to Meals

Many of these herbs are known for their savoury and fragrant properties. They give distinct flavours and an extra punch of taste in whatever dish you decide to use them in.

Don't you fancy some pizza with chopped fresh leaves of basil, parsley, sage, or/and thyme? Will, it is not nice to make your pesto sauce from your basil plants for pasta and sandwiches? Or how about making some salad with basil, cilantro, chives, or mint leaves? Or soups with rosemary, sage, or thyme? Steak with rosemary? There are so many dishes where you can use various types of herbs. You can even come up with your own.

Not only do they make your dishes great, but they are also rich in essential nutrients that our body needs, like antioxidants, vitamins, minerals, essential oils, phytosterols, and other nutrients.

Health Remedies and Care Products

Herbs have gained importance in the healthcare industry, that herbal medicine has become an option where traditional medicine doesn't seem to work. Some come in the form of food supplements or teas for the prevention and treatment of various illnesses. But what better way to take advantage of these properties than when they are freshly harvested? Their medicinal properties came largely from the presence of polyphenols, powerful antioxidants that help prevent or reverse damage in our cells related to aging and lifestyle. (Healthy Foods High in Polyphenols)

Source of Savings

Why spend on herbs, be it dried or fresh, when you can grow them in your backyard? One or two of each kind should be enough to supply your regular herb requirements. If you need more, nothing stops you from growing more.

Accessible

A backyard herb garden or a few planter bags lined along the balcony makes it easily accessible when you need your herbs. Readily available when you need them, in the quantity you need (no waste), and as fresh as you want them to be, what can be better than that? Such is the fun in growing them at home.

Easy to Grow

The good news is, growing herbs is less demanding than growing other plants, making them best for beginners. You can start with oregano, basil, mint, thyme, parsley, chive, sage, rosemary, etc. The chances of you getting disappointed over the outcome are low, as long as you follow the general guidelines.

Good Gift Idea

Are you the type who is fond of giving gifts or tokens to friends? You can share your harvest with them, or you can plant them in small pots so they can grow their own. A nicely packed homemade pesto sauce in a jar or herbal tea that you dried will make any homemaker happy.

Herbs Make a Fragrant Garden

Some herbs give off a strong scent that can make your backyard smell good. Lavender tops the list with its sweet fresh smelling scent that you can smell anywhere near where they are planted. Other fragrant herbs are mint, rosemary, and thyme.

Scents offer such a calming, mood-boosting, stress-reducing, and energizing effect that people are willing to spend on scented candles, scented room spray, incense, and aroma diffuser to get those benefits. (The Hidden Force of Fragrance) Well, you can have it for free with your herb garden.

Herbs Serve as Ornamentals

Lavenders, rosemary, spearmints are flowering herbs that can be decorative. But even with just the different shapes and forms of the various herbs, they can lend themselves as decorative pieces to any garden.

Basil and Thyme

Herbs to Plant in Grow Bags

Now, let's go to the options of herbs to grow.

Herbs from the Mint Family

Many of the better-known herbs belong to the family of Mint (Lamiaceae) like mint, basil, oregano, marjoram, rosemary, thyme, lavender, and sage, etc. They share some properties and growing requirements, so I will discuss those they share here.

Common Characteristics

Aside from basil, which is an annual plant, herbs in the mint family that will be presented here are perennial plants. They are easy to grow, and fragrant because they contain aromatic oils. Lamiaceae plants are widely used as sources of fragrances, culinary and medicinal herbs.

Growing Requirements

All the herbs under the mint family grow best with full sun. Although they are tolerant of some shade, it should not be abused.

They all need well-draining soil as getting their roots soaked is damaging to the plant. The soil should not be overly fertile.

Most can tolerate dry conditions, with some herbs requiring a little bit more water. I will indicate which ones they are in the individual discussion.

Good ventilation is also recommended.

Propagation

They can be grown from seeds and cuttings. You may also buy seedlings that you can transplant in your bags. In the case of rosemary, however, its seeds take a long time to germinate, so you may prefer to use cuttings or buy seedlings instead. The use of cuttings guarantees that you're planting the variety you want.

Pruning

All these herbs benefit from trimming because it makes stems grow for more luscious plants. So frequent harvesting is beneficial. By pruning, you also control their heights.

Time to Plant

Herbs under the family of mint are best planted in spring when there is no chance of frost anymore.

Herbs Belonging to Mint Family

Mint (Mentha)

Mints are hardy and versatile herbs. They grow fast and spread fast too. They produce stems that touch the ground and quickly take roots, called runners. They spread horizontally and can cover your ground easily and overwhelm your other plants. Planting it in a grow bag can limit its spread, but you also must trim runners when they attempt to spill over your bag. They can grow to 1-2 feet, depending on how much you prune them.

Mints need moist but well-drained soil. So you can either water them regularly without making them soggy or use a self-watering tray for your bags.

There are two most used varieties of mints: peppermint and spearmint. Peppermint contains more menthol (40%) than spearmint (0.50%). For culinary applications like drinks, salad, sauces, etc., spearmint is used. Peppermint, on the other hand, is used more for medicinal and hygienic applications. (Difference between Mint, Peppermint, and Spearmint)

Spearmints are added to dishes sparingly because of their strong distinct taste. They contain Vit. A, folate, manganese, and iron. (8 Health Benefits of Mint)

Basil (Ocimum basilicum)

There are many varieties of basil available, but the most used is sweet basil. It has a sweet and savory taste with a hint of mint and anise. It is used in Italian dishes, in sauces, salads, soup, meat, fish dishes, and in the most popular pesto for pasta, sandwiches, dips, pizza, and whatever else you can think of.

It can grow to 12-18 inches, but you can trim it for a bushier and shorter plant. Basil is one among the herbs under the mint family that require a bit more moisture in the soil, but like the other herbs, the water must be well-drained. You can use a self-watering tray to make sure that the soil doesn't dry too much.

Sweet basil is rich in vitamins, minerals, and antioxidants.

Oregano

Oregano (Origanum Vulgare)

Oregano grows to 8 - 24 inches tall and is, intolerant to hot and dry conditions. It is also a spreader that can serve as ground cover.

Widely used in Italian dishes, pasta, meat, salad, etc., its leaves have a pungent earthy sweet taste with a hint of pepper. It can be a little sharp and bitter, which gives dishes a distinct flavour.

Oregano is packed with antioxidants, vitamin K and E, manganese, iron, tryptophan, and calcium. (Why Is Oregano Good for Me?)

Marjoram (Origanum Majorana)

Marjoram is another spreader plant and drought-tolerant like oregano making it perfect for beginners. It grows in clumps, which you can divide to propagate, in addition to the earlier discussed way of propagation. It can grow to up to three feet when not trimmed.

It has a pungent and sweet aroma and has a similar flavour to oregano but milder and has a mildly bitter note. It is used for meat and vegetable dishes.

Rosemary (Rosmarinus Officinalis)

Rosemary is another fragrant herb used in a wide variety of dishes like meats, poultry, fish, soups, steaks, etc. It has quite a strong flavour that is a bit lemony and piney with a bitter note. Its flavour can be a little overpowering.

Rosemary grows well in containers, especially fabric-grow bags, which allow draining of water. It can grow to up to three feet, loves the sun but not the cold, so you can put your bag indoors during the extra cold days.

Thyme (Thymus Vulgaris)

Thyme is another drought-tolerant hardy perennial herb. Too much water can cause its roots to rot and the plant to die.

One herb that blends well with other herbs and spices in cuisines is thyme. It has a subtle minty flavour that can go into any kind of dish without overpowering the other flavours. It goes well in savoury dishes and savoury baking.

Thyme contains vitamins (A & C) and minerals (copper, iron, and manganese)

Sage (Salvia officinalis)

Sage is a hardy perennial plant that grows to about 2 feet tall and 2 feet leave-spread diameter. Like the other herbs from the mint family, sage loves the sun and well-drained soil. It grows well in containers.

Sage goes well in tomato and creamy pasta preparation and many savoury dishes. It is also used as tea. Sage is packed with antioxidants with small amounts of Vitamins (A, C, E), minerals (magnesium, zinc, copper).

* * *

Marjoram, Savia and Lavender

Lavender

English lavenders (Lavandula angustifolia) are the easiest to grow among the many varieties of lavenders. They grow in both hot and cold climates. Like the other herbs in the mint family, lavenders require well-drained, moderately fertile soil. They grow up to up to two feet.

English lavenders are also the most used for culinary purposes with their mild sweet floral taste for drinks, desserts, meats, etc. Their stems and flowers can be used fresh or dried. It is best used with other herbs like oregano, sage, rosemary, etc.

They are widely used for their scent, coming from the essential oil they contain, known herbs are commonly used in perfumes and other personal care products.

Non-Mint Herbs

Parsley (Petroselinum Crispum)

Parsley is from the family of Apiaceae where carrots, celery, coriander/cilantro also belong. They are biennial plants that need a slightly moist loamy soil. It grows well in bags and requires a lot of sun (some shade may be needed in hot areas, though). They are best planted from seeds sown indoors and grown outdoors in early spring.

There are two kinds of parsley: the flat-leafed and curled-leafed, both with distinct flavours, the former having a stronger and more aromatic flavour. They are used as garnishing and to balance flavour in various dishes.

Chives (Allium Schoenoprasum)

Chives are from the onion family. It is a hardy perennial plant that thrives in cool, sunny, and dry areas but can also survive under partial shade. It requires well-drained sandy-loam soil, so it is perfect in grow bags.

Chives are normally planted from the bulb-like known herbs onions and hardly from cuttings in the early spring. The clump can also be divided every few years to propagate.

Chives can go in a variety of dishes. Just cut some leaves when you need some, cut them into small thin pieces to maximize its mild onion flavour, and then add them last in soups and fish and seafood dishes. They are rich in Vits. A, C and K, folate, and manganese, and antioxidants.

Coriander / Cilantro

Coriander, also known as Cilantro, is an annual herb in the family Apiaceae. Like most herbs, they need full sun and well-drained soil.

They can be grown from seeds or from trimmings which you can leave to form roots in a glass of water, after which you can transplant them in your grow bags. Coriander finds itself mostly in Latin American and Asian dishes.

Dill (Anethum graveolens)

Dill is from the same family as parsley and cilantro, Apiaceae, or Umbelliferae, but their flavour is very different from each other. An annual self-seeding herb that grows by itself after each season, some consider it perennial. It prefers full sun, and well-drained and acidic soil, and is cold hardy.

Dill is propagated by directly sowing the seeds in the bag. Transplanting is not recommended as it doesn't like its roots to be disturbed. It is best sown after the last frost. Expect the seeds to germinate in 10-14 days. It can grow to 2-3 feet, but it can be pruned for a shorter and bushier plant.

A versatile plant, you can use its leaves as herbs and its seeds as a spice. Hence, people call them to dill weeds and dill spice accordingly to differentiate. Do they taste the same? Not really, similar but not the same. The flavour of the leaves is similar to parsley and anise with a note of lemon. The seed has the same note of anise and caraway but is more pungent.

Dill Seed Vs. Dill Weed: SPICEography Showdown. It goes well as garnishing in seafood dishes and various kinds of salad.

Growing Herbs Together in Grow Bags

So, you want to grow different kinds of herbs, but you're worried about the space. As mentioned, you can grow some of them together in a container.

There are herbs that you use minimally and those you need regularly, so you can scale depending on your requirements.

In choosing what to grow together, consider the following:

Growing Requirements

Make sure they share the same requirements for the type of soil, amount of sunlight, and water. That way, you can be sure that their growth potential is maximized at the same time.

The following may be grown together as they all prefer it dry: Oregano, Thyme, Marjoram, Rosemary, Sage, Lavender.

Basil and parsley need a little bit more moisture so you can plant them together.

Height of Plants

Having an herb that grows tall faster than others in a bag can block the sun for the other plants, so better choose wisely.

They should grow at the same pace to the same height to avoid overcrowding. Of course, you also do it for aesthetic reasons.

Growing Pattern

Like height, consider their growth pattern. Spreader plants can overwhelm other plants when not controlled. So better not plant mint with other plants as it spreads rather too quickly.

Growing Space

Give each herb the room to grow in the bag, otherwise, they can run to seed when overcrowded like basil and coriander.

Things to Keep in Mind When Growing Herbs in Grow Bags

Rosemary

In addition to what was already stated in this book, and to emphasize some important points necessary in growbag

gardening of herbs, the following are the things to remember to ensure success:

- Use only high-quality soils with minimal fertilization
- The best soil for herbs is the well-draining type as they don't like it soggy. For drought-resistant herbs like rosemary, thyme, oregano, lavender, and sage, you can use the sandier soil so it will drain faster and well. Herbs do not require too fertile soil, for it results in excessive leaf formation and weaker flavour. Mixing some organic soil before planting should be good enough. Fertilize only when extremely necessary after that and only minimally.
- Most herbs do require full sunlight, and for long periods during the day
- Take note of the water requirements of each herb As most herbs do not like too much water, better take note of how long your soil becomes dry to the touch in different weather conditions and set a schedule on when to water them. Use self-watering trays where needed.
- Keep the bags well ventilated
- Take note of the growing pattern of each herb Although some herbs can be grown together in a bag, you have to take care that overcrowding is avoided to make sure each is given room for their growth.

Flowers in Grow Bags

Flowers have an immediate impact on happiness, have long term positive effects on moods, and make intimate connections, according to the study by Jeannette Haviland-Jones, Ph.D. is a professor of psychology at Rutgers University and the director of its Human Emotions Lab. (Rutgers: Flowers Improve Emotional Health). It has even become a symbol of love and affection. People spend on them for gifts and home decoration. A simple wedding can become grand when surrounded by a lot of flowers. Hotels spend millions on them to give warmth to their otherwise cold concrete rooms.

Flowering plants are a good addition to any garden for their colours, scents, and overall aesthetic value. You can plant them directly to the ground, but many opt to have them in containers for versatility. You can move them around for a change in looks or theme.

Aside from all the advantages of grow bags discussed throughout the book, certain flowers do well when cultivated in grow bags, and there are specific reasons for this.

- Flowers don't have extensive root systems
- Flowers do not grow so tall and big as to overwhelm your grow bags
- They can cross-pollinate
- More convenient flower propagation

Flowering Plants Suggestions:

The following are some suggested choices for your flowers in grow bags:

Calla Lilies (Zantedeschia aethiopica)

Calla Lily is one plant that is a joy to have. They are often used as cut flowers used in bouquets and home decorations. They come in white, yellow, pink, purple and black colours.

Calla Lilies are from the family arum. You have a choice between the regular-sized (Zantedeschia aethiopica) or the miniature (Zantedeschia Rehmannii). The former grows up to almost four feet while the latter to only below two feet.

They grow well in most types of containers, with the fabric-grow bags having an advantage because calla lilies require moist but well-drained soil. You can use a self-watering tray to keep the soil moist without making it soggy.

Calla Lily is a perennial plant that grows from a rhizome. It loves full sun but can also grow under partial shade. It is propagated by dividing the rhizomes.

Celosia

If you want bright multi-colours in your garden, you can't go wrong with the celosia of the amaranth family. It is easy to grow – hence not challenging for beginners – in containers as long as you give them a lot of suns and well-draining soil.

It can also survive in partial sun, but that is not the best condition for them.

It comes in various shades of red, pink, orange, and yellow, and three main types: cockscomb, wheat, and plumed. (Crazy, Colorful Celosia: A Growing Guide)

They are annual plants in cool climates but can be perennial in warm conditions. You can easily grow them from seeds, or you can just buy seedlings. To maximize its growth potential, mix some well-balanced organic fertilizer in the soil before putting in the seeds.

Their young leaves are edible and contain vitamins and minerals but harvesting them for this purpose will limit their potential to flower.

Chamomile

Chamomiles are flower plants that are also known for their medicinal characteristics, making them known for chamomile teas from their dried flowers and leaves.

There are two more popular varieties of chamomile, Roman and German chamomiles. Roman variety is an annual plant that produces more fragrant flowers, while the German variety is perennial that produces more flowers. (How to Grow Chamomile).

They grow only to about 2 feet tall and 2 feet leaves-spread diameter when fully grown.

Daffodils

Daffodil (aka Narcissus) is one flower that figures in some songs and poems, and you wonder why of all flowers. Daffodils are said to signify rebirth and new beginnings, as it is one of the first plants that grow at the onset of spring. (Daffodil Meaning and Symbolism)

They are hardy bulb plants, sweet-smelling, and make for great visual enhancement for your balcony throughout spring or autumn. They grow in full sun and partial shade and are not choosy in the soil they can grow in as long as they don't get soggy.

There are many varieties of daffodils, the most popular of which are: trumpet daffodils, large-cupped, small-cupped, doubles, triandrous. (A Beginner's Guide To 13 Types of Daffodils). You will find them in various shades of yellow, white, and orange.

They are planted as bulbs and can survive winter. Some plant them toward the end of autumn so that when spring comes, they are all ready to grow. In bags, you can put three or more bulbs, depending on the size of your bag.

Geranium (Pelargonium)

One flower that is a staple in balcony gardens is Geranium for its bright colours, scent, and the ease by which they are grown. With only up to 5 inches wide clusters, they make for great space savers. They come in red, pink, purple, white, and two-toned.

Geraniums grow well in containers and are even used as hanging plants. They bloom in full sun, but in hot areas, some shade may be beneficial. They require moist and well-draining soil with ample organic matter. Propagation is by cuttings.

Zinnia

If you want some burst of colours in your garden, you can't go wrong with Zinnias. You can have them in white, yellow, orange, red, pink, lavender, and green, and in single, semi-double, and double types, referring to the number of layers of petals in a flower. They grow to 1-3 feet tall with 1-2 feet leaves spread and are ideal as cut flowers. They are attractive to pollinators.

Zinnias are from the family of Asteraceae, with Zinnia Elegans being the most common variety. They are another easy flower to grow, and they grow fast and bloom a lot. They can be propagated by seeds and cuttings.

Zinnia Elegans bloom in full sun and grow best in fertile, well-draining soil.

Pansies (Viola Tricolor hortensis or Viola × Wittrockiana)

Pansies are pretty flowers not only because of their colours but also their design. They resemble butterflies on flowers, or sometimes, faces. From the violet family Violaceae, they come in many different bright colours: white, yellow, gold, orange, red, purple, and deep dark purple, and their combination.

Sadly, for warm areas, pansies prefer the cold climate. They thrive in full sun and partial shade, but it must be cold. They can even survive the frost. They need moist, organic-rich, well-draining soil.

Pansies are perennial but are normally grown as annuals or biennial because they become too tall and leggy during summer. They self-seed as long as the condition is favourable. You can also propagate them by cuttings or dividing a healthy plant from the roots to make two or more rooted plants. They grow well in containers.

Petunia and Geranium

Petunia (Petunia × Atkinsiana)

Petunias are annual plants from the family of Solanaceae. The trumpet-shaped flowers that come in colours white, yellow, pink, red, purple, blue and their combination (gradient, spotted, and stripes) provide a visual delight to any garden.

There are three major categories of petunias based on the size of the flowers: Grandiflora (4"), Multiflora (2"), and Milliflora (1"). (Types of Petunias)

Multiflora is favoured by most gardeners, as it produces more flowers for long periods and is more compact. It is also more resistant to heavy rains.

Multiflora comes in two forms - carpet and wave petunias. The carpet type grows to 8"-10" tall and 12"-36" width and is best for ground covers. Wave petunias, on the other hand, grow to 16"-22" tall and 2'-4' wide. They can also serve as ground cover but also grow well in containers and hanging pots and baskets. Petunias grow best in full sun and any type of well-draining, averagely fertile soil. You can propagate them by cuttings.

Chrysanthemum

Chrysanthemum, also called mums or chrysanths, from the Asteraceae or daisy family, is a herbaceous perennial plant. Its stems die after the end of the growing season, but a new plant grows back from its roots every spring.

They come in single colours of various shades of white, yellow, orange, pink, red, lavender, purple, and bicolour. They are commonly used as cut flowers that can last for up to 2 weeks.

Chrysanthemum grows well in containers, in constantly moist but well-draining organic soil. Full sun will give it its maximum growth potential, but you can also grow them in partial sun. Those that do not get enough sun tend to produce smaller blooms. It grows from 1-3 feet and may need staking to keep them upright.

You can easily propagate them from cuttings from a healthy mature plant and from dividing the plant clump after each growing season. You can extend its blooming season by deadheading.

Hydrangera and Shasta Daisy

Begonias

Begonias from the family of Begoniaceae, are perennial flowering plants that come in many varieties, the most common of which are tuberous and wax begonias. They both produce colourful flowers, but the tuberous variety produces big blooms while wax begonia produces small ones.

Tuberous begonias come in shades of white, yellow, orange, pink, red, and in single, double, ruffled, or toothed forms. They also come in upright and trailing types. (HOW TO GROW & CARE FOR BEAUTIFUL BEGONIAS). They prefer less heat and more shade. The trailing type is best for hanging bags which I will discuss in the next section.

Wax begonia flowers, on the other hand, come in shades of white, blush, pink, rose, bi-colour, scarlet and deep red. They grow in both sun and shade.

Both varieties prefer light, rich, and well-draining soil, never in soggy condition. They can be propagated by letting a healthy stem cutting form roots in a glass of clean water and then transplanting them to the bags.

Angelonia (Angelonia angustifolia)

Angelonia, also known as Summer Snapdragon, is a member of the Plantaginaceae family. Its flowers come in spike form at the top of the stem in white, pink, blue, mauve, and purple colours.

It is a perennial plant but is mostly grown as an annual. It is root-hardy that even if the plant freezes on top, its roots are not affected and can sprout again when spring comes.

It thrives in full sun and partial shade and well-draining slightly acidic soil. It is easy to grow for beginners because they are drought-resistant and do not need deadheading. They grow up to 18 inches tall.

Angelonia is easy to propagate using stem cuttings or by root division. But you can also grow it from seeds when the time of the last frost is nearing.

Nemesia (Nemesia Strumosa)

Nemesia of the Scrophulariaceae family is an annual or perennial flowering plant depending on the variety. They come as sparsely branched plants that produce colourful small, scented clusters of flowers in shades of white, yellow, pink, red, and purple. They grow up to 12-20 inches. They are mostly planted as bedding plants but also grow well in containers.

They grow well in rich, well-draining, slightly acidic soil under full sun or partial sun but are affected by extreme heat. All spent flowers must be removed to encourage more blooming.

You can propagate Nemesia from seeds or through stem cuttings after the last frost is over.

Lobelia (Lobelia Erinus)

Lobelias from the family of Campanulaceae or bellflower are perennial plants that are often grown as annual plants. They produce abundant dainty flowers in shades of white, pink, violet, blue or bicoloured from spring through fall. They are one of the staples in any flower garden because of their long flowering season. Pinching is often done during the early spring to ensure more flower production.

Lobelias are warm-season plants that come in two types: compact lobelia and trailing lobelias. Compact lobelias are best for garden edging, while the trailing type is best for container growing. They are preferred in bringing colours to your window boxes and hanging grow bags. Lobelia Erinus is a trailing type.

They grow in rich, well-drained but moist soil, in full sun but can tolerate partial shade. They can be propagated from seeds and new stems after the last frost.

Vervain

Vervain, also known as verbena, of the family of Verbenaceae, is one easy plant to grow and is perfect for grow-bag gardening. Like most flowering plants, they grow well in full sun and well-draining soil. They are annual plants that self-seed hence are mistaken as perennial. They are also drought tolerant.

They come in various varieties, low-growing upright and trailing. The trailing type is best for pots and hanging bags. Vervain flowers come in white, pink, red, violet, and blue colours in clusters, and the blooming season can last from spring until close to frost.

You can sow its seeds nearing the end of the frost and be transplanted in spring. The seeds take about a month to germinate, however.

Hanging Grow Bags

We must all be familiar with hanging flower baskets and pots, but hanging grow bags? Yes, there are grow bags specifically made for hanging. They come in rectangular, usually narrow, bags with holes or pockets on the sides where you can plant your flowering plants. When they are already firmly planted, you can hang them on your porch, balcony, outdoor wall, fence, lamp posts, under the tree, etc. for some beautiful cascading layers of colourful flowers. (Hanging Grow Bags).

Hanging grow bags allow you to maximize space even more. You can plant different flowers on each bag or the same plant in different colours for a multi-coloured ensemble. Pansies and petunias are two of the flowers that you can start with. The trailing variety of flowers is best for this purpose.

Like in ordinary grow bags, you must consider the growing requirements of the plant, and if you're going to mix plants in a bag, make sure that they share the same growing requirements.

Things to Keep in Mind in Grow Bag Gardening

You must be excited by now to start your herbs and flower garden. Wait, not too fast. Here are some points to remember before you start to avoid wasting your time and resources and avoid disappointments.

- Think out what you want to achieve, like the plants you want to grow. Your choice of plants and their varieties must take into consideration the following:
- Growing requirements of the plant/variety
- The climate in your location, choose the best-suited plant and variety
- The size of your space
- The amount of sun that you get in your space – morning and afternoon sun
- Decide on the size of your bags based on the available space and the garden design that you want to achieve. Do you plan to move them around? If so, then you must consider the ease of moving them.
- Follow the guidelines on the type of soil, the amount of sun, water, and fertilizer.
- Follow the recommended planting time to ensure success.

- Adhere to the planting and caring guidelines. Make sure you wet the roots o the bottom of the bag when you water them but make sure not to soak them. Most herbs and flower plants don't like soggy soil.
- When you encounter problems with the plants, read on the possible problem and solution for more guided steps.

I think we have covered the basics of herbs and flower grow-bag gardening. I look forward to hearing about your gardening journey someday.

GLOSSARY

Acidic: property of a material with high acid content; material with a pH value of 1-6

Aeration: introduction of air into a mixture

Air layering: also known as marcotting; a method of propagating plants by peeling the bark of a stem and then wrapping the exposed wood with a moist rooting media like moss and plastic sheet

Annual plants: plants that complete their life span in a single growing season

Air pruning: the natural phenomenon of roots drying when exposed to dry air preventing overly wound-up roots in containers

Aquaponics: growing plants in the water together with fish providing a symbiotic environment. The plants benefit from the discharge of the fish and the fish from the cleaned water by the plant

Biennial plants: plants that complete their life cycle in two growing seasons

Biodegradable: property of the material that decays naturally by the action of microorganisms

Black gold: also known as compost, are a mixture of decayed plants and organic wastes used as fertilizer

Breathable: property of a material to describe its ability to allow air and liquid to pass through its pores

Climate change: the rise in global temperature brought about by gas emissions in the environment

Coconut coir: fibrous part from coconut husk

Compost: a mixture of decayed plants and organic wastes used as fertilizer; it is also known as black gold

Compost bin: container where organic refuse is dumped for composting purposes

Composting: a process of allowing waste materials such as leaves, woods, and food scraps to decay together for fertilizer use

Container gardening: growing plants in pots, cans, plastic bags, pails, grow bags, and other containers instead of directly in the ground

Cuttings: parts of the plant (stem, leaves, roots) that are capable of growing into a new plant

Deadheading: the practice of removing spent flowers from the plant for improved appearance and to promote continued bloom

Dehydration: lack of water from too little watering or too hot weather

Drip system: also known as drip irrigation is a method of watering the plants directly from the water source to the plants through pipes, valves, and emitters. As the name implies, the water is delivered in drips.

Emitters: device connected to the pipe or hose that sprinkle or spray the water to the plant, e.g., nozzle

Fertilizer: a substance, synthetic or natural, added to the soil to improve its fertility

Germination: the natural process by which a plant grows from a seed

GMO: or Genetically Modified Organisms are plants, animals, or other organisms the genetic make-up of which has been altered in the laboratory to change some of their characteristics

Green thumb: natural talent in growing plants

Grow bag: thick breathable fabric bag used as a container for planting

Hardy plants: plants that can survive cold weather

Herbs: plants with aromatic and savoury properties used for flavouring and medicinal purposes

Hydroponic: a way of growing plants in nutrient-rich water without soil

In-ground gardening: traditional growing of plants directly in the ground

Inorganic fertilizer: also called commercial and synthetic fertilizers; chemically manufactured fertilizer from petroleum products or naturally occurring minerals

Interplanting: also known as intercropping; the practice of growing more than one plant at the same time. They can have different growth rates and nutrient requirements so they will not have to compete. It is a way to maximize a space

Landscape fabric: material placed on top of the soil in a given space or around the plant to control the weeds from growing by limiting their exposure to the sun which they need for their growth

Macronutrients: nutrients used by plants in big amounts such as Nitrogen, Phosphorus, and Potassium (commonly known by their chemical symbol N, P, K, respectively) and Sulfur, Calcium, and Magnesium

Micronutrients: nutrients used by plants in small amounts such as Manganese, Boron, Copper, Iron, Molybdenum, Zinc, Chlorine, Cobalt, Silicon

Molasses: thick black syrup that is a by-product of sugar refining

Mulching: the practice of covering the soil, often around the plant, with leaves, bark, or compost to protect the roots of the plant from too much heat or cold, to prevent the growth of weeds, or to add nutrients to the soil

Non-GMO: or Non-genetically Modified Organisms are plants, animals, or other organisms with an unaltered genetic make-up

Olla: a simple, unglazed pot

Organic fertilizer: plant- or animal-based materials that are either a by-product or end product of naturally occurring processes, such as animal manure and composted organic materials.

Organic waste: biodegradable waste from plants and animals

Oxygenation: the process of adding oxygen to anything

Pathogens: microorganisms that can cause diseases

Peat moss: fibrous material from partially decayed plant remains

Perennial plants: plants that complete their life cycle in more than two years

Perlite: crushed volcanic materials; it makes a porous bed for fast-draining soil mix

pH: a measure of acidity and alkalinity of a substance (water, soil, etc.) represented by numbers 1 to 14, 1 being the most acidic, 7 as neutral, and 14 as most alkaline

Photosynthesis: the process by which green plants use sunlight to convert water, and carbon dioxide to oxygen for the environment and carbohydrates for the growth of the plant

Pinching: a form of pruning that involves cutting from the tip of the plant to encourage branching

Polyester: a type of plastic that can be made into thread, fabric, films, and other plastic items

Polypropylene: a type of plastic that can be made into thread, yarn, fabric, film, and other forms

Potting mix: a sterile soilless mixture of materials used in container gardening

Potting soil: a mixture of peat moss, ground bark and may or may not contain soil

Propagation: the process of producing new plants from seeds, stems, roots, or leaves

Pruning: cutting of some parts of the plant to control its growth and development

Raised beds garden: also known as garden boxes; an elevated garden that is often enclosed by wood, concrete, or rocks

Rootball: the whole mass of roots and soil that shows when you remove a plant from a container or the soil

Root-bound: when roots become too dense and entangled that there is no more room for the roots to grow in like when planted in containers for so long

Runners: stems that touch the ground and quickly take roots causing the lateral spread of the plant

Seedling: young plant grown from a seed

Self-sow: the natural process by which new plants are produced from seeds that drop to the

ground from an old plant

Self-watering grow bags: placing of a shallow container with water under the bag for a continuous supply of water to the soil

Slow-release fertilizer: a kind of fertilizer that releases nutrients to the soil in a continuous slow fashion either by the natural decomposition of organic materials or by the slow breakdown of the fertilizer coating

Spreader: plants that grow laterally and cover the ground

Square foot gardening: a kind of raised bed garden that plants densely in squares

Succulents: plants with stems and leaves that can store a lot of water (eg. cacti) making them drought resistant

Suckers: plants that grow beside the parent plant from its lateral roots or stems (eg. bananas)

Transplant: to transfer a plant, normally seedlings, from one place to another

Trellis: framework made of wood, bamboo, or metal used to support climbing plants

Vermiculite: naturally occurring light mineral that is added to the soil for aeration and water retention

Vertical gardening: growing plants in a vertically positioned structure usually placed against the wall or fence. This is usually done to maximize space and for aesthetic purposes

Webbing: a strong strip of fabric woven flat or in tube form used in place of ropes. They are usually used as a handle of bags

Weeds: undesirable plants that grow with and competing for nutrients with the desired plants

Leave a 1- Click Review !

Customer Reviews

★★★★★ 2

5.0 out of 5 stars ▾

5 stars		100 %
4 stars		0%
3 stars		0%
2 stars		0%
1 stars		0%

See all verified purchase reviews ▸

Share your thoughts with other customers

Write a Customer Reviews

I would be incredibly thankful if you could take just 60 seconds to write a brief review on Amazon, even if it's just a few sentences!

Scan the QR code below to leave your review:

CONCLUSION

Sunflowers

To someone who's a newbie at gardening, planting in grow bags might be daunting. Sure, it'll be a challenging journey. You'll have hiccups along the way. But don't worry. You're not alone. Let this book guide you. It has everything you need from start to finish.

If you need a refresher on any of the topics in this book, from starting your grow bag garden to cultivating many different plants, just reread the chapters.

Here's to a happy, exciting, and productive grow bag gardening! I'm rooting for you!

RESOURCES

Wood and Garden: www.cambridge.org/jp/academic/subjects/life-sciences/plant-science/wood-and-garden-notes-and-thoughts-practical-and-critical-working-amateur

Cabaus: https://cabaus.org/2015/03/20/5-ways-gardening-can-reduce-your-carbon-footprint/

Evidence-Gardening for health: a regular dose of gardening: www.ncbi.nlm.nih.gov/pmc/articles/PMC6334070/

National Garden Bureau: www.growertalks.com/Article/?articleid=20101

Treehugger: www.treehugger.com/great-gardening-websites-4858719

North Dakota State University: www.ag.ndsu.edu/publications/lawns-gardens-trees/the-facts-of-square-foot-gardening

Gardeningknowhow: www.gardeningknowhow.com/

plant-problems/environmental/temperature-on-plants.htm

Greenupside: https://greenupside.com/how-long-do-grow-bags-last/

Deptswashington: https://depts.washington.edu/propplnt/Chapters/air-pruning.htm

Worldagroforestry: https://blog.worldagroforestry.org/index.php/2013/08/20/biodegradable-seedling-bags-could-grow-stronger-trees-but-can-they-replace-polythene/

Growinginthegarden.com: https://growinginthegarden.com/gardening-in-grow-bags-5-tips-for-success/

Healthline: www.healthline.com/health/is-polypropylene-safe%23bottom-line

Naturaler: https://naturaler.co.uk/is-polypropylene-biodegradable/

Empressofdirt: http://empressofdirt.net/sew-grow-bags/#sizes.

How to Make Grow Bags - You Tube: www.youtube.com/watch?v=oc-2DDbL4kE

Greenupside: https://greenupside.com/what-can-you-grow-in-a-grow-bag/

Urban survival site: https://urbansurvivalsite.com/fruits-and-veggies-you-can-grow-in-buckets/

Northernhomestead: https://northernhomestead.com/when-to-plant-what/

https://northernhomestead.com/soil-for-container-gardening-and-raised-beds/

https://northernhomestead.com/grow-grow-bags/

https://northernhomestead.com/soil-for-container-gardening-and-raised-beds/

https://northernhomestead.com/?s=sew+grow+bag

https://northernhomestead.com/soil-for-container-gardening-and-raised-beds/

Thespruce: www.thespruce.com/what-is-a-soilless-potting-mix-1403085

www.thespruce.com/difference-between-potting-soil-potting-mix-847812

www.thespruce.com/common-container-gardening-mistakes-847796

The Better india: www.thebetterindia.com/195035/lifestyle-home-garden-tips-how-to-pot-plant-seed-compost-guide-india/

Home Guides: https://homeguides.sfgate.com/daylight-hours-grow-lettuce-70987.html

Grow Journey: www.growjourney.com/finally-garden-pot-sizes-decoded/#potsizetable

Homestratosphere: www.homestratosphere.com/what-can-i-use-to-fill-the-bottom-of-a-large-planter/

Journelssagepub: https://journals.sagepub.com/doi/abs/10.1177/1359105310365577

Researchgate:
www.researchgate.net/publication/331493537_Benefits_of_Gardening_Activities

_for_Cognitive_Function_According_to_Measurement_of_Brain_Nerve_Growth_Factor_Levels

Health line: www.healthline.com/nutrition/benefits-of-cauliflower%23TOC_TITLE_HDR_2

www.healthline.com/nutrition/mint-benefits

Webmd: www.webmd.com/diet/foods-high-in-polyphenols%231#1

www.webmd.com/food-recipes/features/why-is-oregano-good-for-me%23:~:text=Fresh%2520oregano%2520is%2520a%2520great,vitamin%2520E,%2520tryptophan%2520and%2520calcium.

Psychology today: www.psychologytoday.com/intl/articles/200711/the-hidden-force-fragrance

Theydiffer: https://theydiffer.com/difference-between-mint-peppermint-and-spearmint/

Safnow: https://safnow.org/aboutflowers/quick-links/health-benefits-research/emotional-impact-of-flowers-study/

Gardenerspath: https://gardenerspath.com/plants/annuals/celosia/

Ftd: www.ftd.com/blog/share/daffodil-meaning-and-symbolism

Herebydesign: https://herebydesign.net/a-beginners-guide-to-the-different-types-of-daffodils/

Dengarden: https://dengarden.com/gardening/petunia-flower

Gardendesign: www.gardendesign.com/plants/begonia.html

Hanging Grow Bags - You Tube: www.youtube.com/watch?v=sGfgd3y5jQ

Printed in Great Britain
by Amazon

81681448R00116